The
7 Greatest
Truths About
Successful
Women

Marion Luna Brem

G. P. PUTNAM'S SONS

NEW YORK

The
7 Greatest
Truths About
Successful
Women

*How You Can Achieve
Financial Independence,
Professional Freedom,
and Personal Joy*

Many of the names, identifying characteristics, and other relevant details of the anecdotal cases in this book have been modified to protect the privacy of these individuals. Some cases are composites, also disguised.

G. P. Putnam's Sons
Publishers Since 1838
a member of
Penguin Putnam Inc.
375 Hudson St.
New York, NY 10014

Library of Congress Cataloging-in-Publication Data

Brem, Marion Luna.
The 7 greatest truths about successful women :
how you can achieve financial independence, professional
freedom, and personal joy / Marion Luna Brem.
p.   cm.
ISBN 0-399-14743-8
1. Success in business.   2. Businesswomen.   I. Title:
Seven greatest truths about successful women.   II. Title.
HF5386 .B814   2001   2001019324
650.1'082—dc21

Printed in the United States of America
1   3   5   7   9   10   8   6   4   2

This book is printed on acid-free paper. ♾

Book design by Amanda Dewey

This book is dedicated to my two sons,
Brannon Brem and Travis Brem.

acknowledgments

Thank you, John Boswell, for your forward thinking, and for bringing me to John Duff. Thank you, John Duff, for helping me tap into all of my strengths and for sharing some of your own, especially creativity. And thank you to the rest of the amazing team at Penguin Putnam.

Thank you to the many female entrepreneurs described in this book who shared their inspiring stories.

Thank you, Susan Luna, for introducing me to my resiliency. Thank you, Gracie Perez, for sharing all of my passions in business but mostly my passion to write this book.

Thank you, Kathryn Childers, for helping me think big. Thank you, Tim Fitzmorris, for helping me with the personal side of balance and leadership. Thank you, Mike Waddell, Sarah Hills, Maricela Pappas, and Jessica Williams, for nurturing me through much of the process.

Thank you, Audrey Ellzey and Whitney Rogers, for your sweet intuition.

Thank you, Rusty Williams and the rest of my team at Love Chrysler and Love Chrysler Dodge Jeep, for minding the stores so that I could take time off to write this book.

Thank you, Pa, for encouraging me to keep climbing, even when I was tired.

And finally, thank you, Mom, for teaching me to believe in myself.

contents

Part 1

Part 2

Part 1

one

Who Wants to Be Her Own Boss?

I've been called a survivor. In truth, I'm not living life to survive. I'm living life to thrive. Every day I celebrate what has been called my "indomitable spirit." I have overcome tremendous obstacles to realize my dreams and I feel inspired to help you do the same.

My accomplishments have been described as "incredible." They have been measured in revenues, numbers of employees, and even awards. But what can't be measured in any of us is passion, that certain fire in the heart that ignites courage. If you have a passion to lift up your life and the life of your family, I'm glad this book has joined us together.

My own struggles and successes have given me a certain perspective on women's strengths *and* weaknesses. Becoming aware of what they are is the first step we'll be taking together. It's a given. Unless you recognize and understand your strengths, you cannot maximize them. Unless you embrace your perceived weaknesses, you cannot minimize them or turn them to your advantage.

In this postfeminist era, I think it is safe to assume that the world at large accepts the fact that there are basic differences between men and women that go well beyond biology. My contention is that a woman's attributes as well as her shortcomings all conspire to make us, in general, more attuned to and adept at entrepreneurship than men.

But rest assured. This is *not* just another use-your-feminine-wiles book. (Batting your eyelashes went out with corsets and high-button shoes.) Nor is it a do-it-like-the-guys playbook. Though I do not blame men for writing the rules (considering they were the only ones playing the game for a long time), I believe we've been too intent on trying to do it "by the book." What women are coming to realize is that they can be the authors of their *own* book!

From high-tech to high-rise, in the following chapters you'll read numerous anything-is-possible tales, all of them a salute to the female entrepreneurial spirit. The stories of the dynamic women you'll meet in these pages reveal that there are many doors into the business world and many opportunities to grow and change in your present situation. For some of these women, their motivation came from a little voice inside that said, "I feel a calling to fill a need." For others, it was a calling to meet their own needs—simply to pay the bills or to combat boredom or to overcome a lack of fulfillment in their present jobs. Some wanted to earn respect. Some wanted to earn money. Most wanted to earn both.

Linda Denny, the national director for the Women's Market for ING Aetna Financial Services, has been in the business of recruiting women both as customers and agents. She has traveled around the country for more than two decades— almost like a traveling road show—not only to sell women retirement plans but also to sell them on the idea of having independent careers. Her research has revealed a fundamental difference in men and women when it comes to their career goals.

In her recruitment efforts, Ms. Denny has conducted controlled focus groups asking both men and women to identify what they respectively value in a job or career. According to her research, men's number one priority is how much money they can make. Women also claim that money is their first priority but it's not a matter of *how much* but *how secure* their paycheck will be.

But in light of our current economic and business climate, it's clear that there is no security where there is no control.

In my experience, control is about having the courage to

set your own priorities—to balance your professional ambitions with your personal life.

I chose sales in a male-dominated industry as my career path. My rapid ascent from becoming the first saleswoman ever hired by that particular car dealership to the CEO of four businesses, including two car dealerships (one of which is the largest of its kind in the state of Texas), is a unique but not unusual story. I did not inherit money. I did not have any access to any "special programs." What I did have was the determination to pull myself up by my bootstraps, as they say in Texas.

Today my business enterprise is ranked high on the list of The Top 500 Women-Owned Businesses in America. I'm proud of my success but mostly I'm proud that I have been able to define my success. For me, earning money is not just about economic power. It's about having more choices, pride in accomplishment, flexibility, and freedom. It's about taking control of my life.

Two years ago I was honored to win the Avon Women of Enterprise Award, which is given to four women each year by the Avon Corporation. Because of this, I've had the privilege of meeting many of Avon's best. These include Vondell McKenzie, whose own story is well worth hearing.

As a child, Vondell witnessed her father's business literally go up in smoke. His auto repair shop, a product of his own entrepreneurial dream, was intentionally burned to the ground because he refused to relinquish the prime property on which it sat. She learned about courage firsthand, as she saw her father start over and rebuild the business.

As an adult, she married a loving man and together they raised their three children. Though she was looking forward to her husband's retirement, she was not looking forward to "pinching pennies." And so she started an Avon business. She went door to door asking her neighbors if they were interested in buying Avon products but she didn't stop there. She also asked them if they were interested in *selling* Avon products! She thus helped pioneer a new business concept for Avon, which is now part of their Leadership Program.

Not only did Vondell's Avon business bring the family the income they wanted once her husband retired, but he even got involved. For five years, until he died of cancer, he proudly took on the role as her chauffeur.

Today, Vondell finds comfort knowing that her flexible schedule made it possible for her to nurture her husband in his last months of illness while operating her business out of her home office. She listens to her inner voice as she looks to the future, but right now she's content to manage her $5.5 million Avon empire in memory of her husband.

I'll share more of my own story with you in the coming chapters: how I was also faced with an unexpected life change, and how a peek at death helped me realize that courage is not a gift granted to a few. As I discovered, courage is a decision! You have to wake up each morning with a simple declaration; "Today I'm going to be courageous."

We're afraid of rejection. We're afraid of the unknown. We're afraid of making fools of ourselves. Some of us may even be afraid of success. It takes courage not to be afraid.

The truth is that your fears are real. Corporations downsize. New businesses fail at an alarming rate. Unexpected circumstances upset even the best-laid plans. But through the experiences of the women in this book you'll discover a cache of resources—those special feminine attributes that you have at your disposal.

As a resourceful woman, you no longer have to curb your ambitions. It's time to cast off your own sense of limits and understand that you don't have to know *everything* to take the plunge. You *can* learn while doing. (I did. I still am.)

As an entrepreneur, I promise you will have the love and support of others just like you. Women have always been good at sharing and now they're sharing a whole lot more than casserole recipes. You won't be alone. You'll be in a community of women currently 9.1 million strong who are contributing almost $4 trillion to our economy! That's almost double what it was just twelve years ago. (Most of that growth has taken place in the last three years.) Much of the pioneering has been done. Much of the road has been paved. But there are still many miles to travel.

This book is about sharing tried-and-true recipes for success. But best of all, with the inspiration and practical guidance within its pages, you'll be able to decide on which ingredients are right for you. My sincerest wish is that you will be inspired to tap into your own creativity to sell yourself a life of financial independence, professional freedom, and personal joy.

two

Ladies, Start
Your Engines

I had been hugging the toilet most of the day. The cold
porcelain felt good against my cheek. It was hard to imagine that the chemo drugs that had been pumped into my veins
for months were doing any good. How could anything this
horrible be good for you? And they call this a "side effect"?

As I lay there, I could hear my sons crashing about in the
kitchen. Then I smelled something burning. My twelve-year-
old, with his seven-year-old brother a half a step behind him,
appeared at the bathroom door holding a smoking pan of
macaroni and cheese. "Don't worry, Mom," the oldest said

with confidence, "only the bottom is burned. The top part is still good." I knew right then that dying was not an option. My sons needed me. And I pulled myself up from the floor to face my future.

If there's such a thing in life as a defining moment, seeing my two boys with a panful of charred macaroni and cheese was certainly mine. But in reality, the dawn of realization of what I had to do did not just suddenly appear. A long dark night had led up to it.

Eight months earlier, the partially masked face of an aqua-eyed, middle-aged man with a tanned forehead came to me out of the fog of anesthesia. "Well, Doctor, was it something exotic?" I asked.

"No. It was good old run-of-the-mill cancer," he replied. "We had to take the left breast and your lymph nodes."

Only the day before he had assured me that it couldn't possibly be cancer. After all, I didn't fit the profile. I had no family history of breast cancer. Barely thirty years of age, I was too young for breast cancer. The tumor (later ironically referred to as a "man-eater") was too large to be malignant because if it had been, the doctor had assured me, I wouldn't have been alive. It had to be something "exotic."

I asked to have a moment to myself before they let my family in to see me. I thought of my mother first. I wanted her special maternal comforting and strength that had seen me through childhood illness, accident, and heartbreak. Little did I know that when she'd heard the news about my cancer, she had to be sedated and taken home. My prognosis was grim. "Two to five years to live," the surgeon had told her. For the time being anyway, it seemed I would have to nurture myself.

It wouldn't be easy. Only weeks earlier I had undergone a hysterectomy for cervical cancer. Now I lay in another recovery room asking myself, "Haven't I already been through more than my share? No, don't go there. Be strong. Your family needs you."

Highly toxic, grueling chemotherapy followed. I vividly recall my first visit to the oncologist to get my first dose. I was escorted by my mother, who had risen to the occasion once she got past the initial shock of my prognosis, and best friend, Susan. I wore a vibrant red blouse with a large left pocket to disguise my missing breast and carried a small pillow under my arm to guard the wound. With a touch of makeup and my hair styled, believe it or not, I thought I looked pretty good. But when I saw the waiting room full of frail, sickly looking cancer patients with pale yellow complexions and bald heads, I bolted! It took another twenty-four hours for my mother and Susan to get through to me, and I returned for my first lifesaving chemo treatment.

Several months into chemo, my marriage gave way under the strain. Newly separated with my two young sons to care for, I guess you could say that I was at a real low point. I had lost my ability to bear children, lost a breast, lost my hair, lost my *Leave It to Beaver* home life. But above all, I had lost my sense of self-worth.

Again, I turned to my best friend, Susan, who had been with me throughout the whole ordeal. "Susan, what am I going to do? How am I going to find a job with nothing but a homemaker's résumé?" I almost cried. I had so little experience in the "real" world.

She patiently reminded me that "homemaking experience" meant much more than cleaning and changing diapers. It meant managing time and money, setting priorities, planning space, and lots of other valuable skills that could be used in the workplace. Her words pulled me out of my funk and got me thinking about what I had to offer. "And you've always been good with people," she said. "Why don't you try sales?"

I was desperate and ready to cling to any life ring that was thrown my way. With the equivalent of a death sentence hanging over me, I didn't have a lot of time. My boys needed me and I had to figure out what to do. With whatever spark of a passion for living that remained, and a few well-timed words of advice from a good friend, I saw some signs of hope.

Though I was still a bit weak from the chemotherapy, I tried to make up in enthusiasm what I lacked in energy. I willed myself to change my self-talk from "I think I can" to "I know I will" and with a prosthesis tucked inside my bra and a cheap wig on my head to disguise my chemo-induced baldness, I knocked on my first door.

For most women, that first door seemed an unlikely choice—the showroom of a local car dealership. Years earlier, in one of my few jobs outside the home, I had worked as a telephone receptionist in a dealership. So I figured that my familiarity with the lingo of the place would at least open the door.

Well, I didn't even get my foot in that first door. Two weeks and sixteen doors later, sitting in my car outside yet another dealership, I wiped my tear-diluted mascara, stroked on some fresh lipstick, looked at myself in the rearview mirror, and mustered up the gumption for one more go. Though it was hard, I had been trying not to take these rejections personally. I reminded myself that these guys don't know me. They don't know what I have to offer, and, most important, they don't know what they're missing. During those two weeks, I came to realize that I needed to change not only the way I was thinking about my situation but also the way that I presented myself to prospective employers. I had never gotten anywhere playing the victim and that certainly wasn't going to change now. So I determined to change my pitch from "Have you ever thought about hiring a woman to sell cars?" to "Here's what I think I can do for you."

Bingo! The next sales manager looked straight at me and said—and I swear these were his exact words—"I've been thinking about hiring a broad." And he did.

As I walked, or should I say skipped, out to the car, my wig almost fell off. I didn't care. Actually, I felt like flinging that sucker up to the sky—but I didn't. Instead, I started my engine and raced home to tell my sons the good news. Not even the speeding ticket I got on my way home could lessen my feelings of *"Yes!"*

Five Beautiful Truths About Women

Even though I hadn't set out to reinvent my life, I knew that I was going to have to find the courage to do what I needed to do. Though I was motivated by the love and needs of my family, it took *me* to make the decision. I had two choices: I could give up or I could give it my all. But what was "my all"?

I needed to overcome the challenges that I faced. I had to figure out how to do it with the limited resources I thought I had. As I searched deep inside myself to find them, I discovered a remarkable reservoir of strengths that I never recognized before. (And a couple of weaknesses surfaced that could have sabotaged everything that I was trying to do. But I'll talk about those later on.) This was more insight than I was looking for as I clung to the toilet retching my guts out. Over the years since then I've come to think that I share these strengths with most women. And while they are not restricted to the females of our species, there is something about them that speaks particularly to our hearts.

Even in the depths of my despair, something was keeping me going. Some call it a will to survive. Others call it an indomitable spirit. Whatever it was, it acted like a spring, giving me the ability to bounce back from a very low place. I think of it as a resiliency, and it's the first truth about women that came to mind throughout my personal ordeal and one that I've discovered is shared by countless women who find themselves in difficult situations.

I've never considered myself to be a completely selfless person or anything like a martyr but it seemed to me that no matter what was happening to me, I was always trying to spare others. In spite of the temporary lapse when I went for my first chemo treatments, most of the time I would act tough when I didn't feel tough—for the sake of my loved ones. Sometimes my "act" would be played on people I hardly knew. I remember how I tried to make it easier on the doctors and nurses. I found myself telling them not to worry about me, to spend their time with the other patients. It wasn't that I was in a state of denial, I was in a state of caregiving. My maternal instincts were kicking in. While I appreciate that many men share this quality of nurturing, the truth is that women are, by nature, the nurturers of the world.

If nurturing is the second truth, the third springs from the old cliché about women's intuition. I am not a person who embraces New Age concepts unreservedly. I am too much of a pragmatist for that. But once I got past thinking about my own precarious state of physical and mental health, I gave myself over to the idea that if something felt right, I would act on it. My friend's recommendation that I look for work in sales was the thing that felt right to me. Choosing the car business may have seemed counterintuitive to most people. Why should I set myself up for disappointment and rejection from such a male-dominated business? As it turned out, and pretty successfully I think, I followed my own intuition about what I could and needed to do. That gut feeling, or whatever you choose to call it, is something that most women will follow even when the facts may appear to get in the way.

Just like when I was a little girl playing dolls and dress-up, as an adult I needed to unleash my inner child to imagine the life I could have. With a little help from my friends, I created a whole new picture in my mind of my future. And this was no paint-by-numbers project, believe me. Not only did I have to envision myself as a successful sales executive (the fact that I didn't stop at just being a good car salesperson isn't lost on me now), but also I had to believe in a life beyond the two to five years of my prognosis. My reinvention required all of the creativity I could come up with. It's remarkable how expansive my imagined life became when unfettered by the reality of how I was going to get there. If, as a young girl, I could imagine having tea with the Queen of England or marrying Prince Charming, then why not create the scene in which I hand over the keys to a shiny new car to my first buyer. Reality has a way of interfering with creativity so I chose to ignore it in order to get through those first trying days.

The resiliency I demonstrated, the nurturing side of myself I revealed, the intuition I activated, and the creativity I cultivated, all conspired to become a mighty force because of my passion. My passion to live and thrive—not just to survive—and my passion for continuing on with the awesome responsibility of mothering gave birth to my new passion—to change my circumstances. Passion, like love, is not a word with which most men are comfortable. Perhaps they confuse passion with lust. Lust in a woman does not sound like an attractive trait. But passion, when we find the courage to unleash it, is a most powerful motivator and a truth that women are not afraid to express.

Two Not-So-Beautiful Truths About Women

I feel compelled to share with you what appeared in my road to recovery as a couple of potholes, or roadblocks. These shortcomings, or challenges, are known by different names but I call them low self-value and oversensitivity. These traits are embarrassingly common to women. I dare say that a woman can have all the talent, ability, and wherewithal in the world, but if she doesn't get a firm grip on these two short-comings, she's not apt to get very far. I'll get into these more deeply in Part 3, but by way of introduction, let me give you my feelings and observations in a nutshell.

When it comes to wanting others to place value on us, first we better be sure we're placing it on ourselves. If we feel like we deserve only crumbs, how can we expect that someone will offer us a whole loaf? And when we allow others to define who we are, we lose our sense of self altogether.

Low self-value leads to the second of the two not-so-beautiful truths about women: oversensitivity. My credentials to write on this subject are unquestionable. I have my mother's DNA and that makes me an emotional hemophiliac (I hope that doesn't hurt her feelings too badly). There's no better way to become a slave to the opinions and needs of others than to be overly sensitive. When you let your feelings become the CEO of your life, the ruler of your world, you give up tremendous power. I believe it is the main reason that women suffer ridicule and exclusion in the workplace. Men may lack the sensitivity to deal with a woman who expresses her feelings, but so long as there remains a separation of the *state of business* and the *religion of emotions* in the business world, women will have to learn not to take everything so personally. It doesn't mean that women need to act "more like a man," as the character Henry Higgins in *Pygmalion* (*My Fair Lady* for those more familiar with the popular stage and movie versions of the story) would have us believe. Eliza Doolittle triumphed specifically because she learned to overcome her low self-esteem and overly sensitive responses to Professor Higgins's bullying. She understood the beautiful truths about women and used them to her own ends.

I discovered the validity of the seven truths about myself as a result of soul searching. And I have come to learn that I am not alone. I don't have exclusive ownership of any of these strengths or weaknesses. My observations and experience working with hundreds of women in sometimes emotionally and financially intimate situations have reinforced this discovery. Chances are you are resilient, nurturing, intuitive, creative, and passionate. Perhaps you just haven't let yourself believe it because you've been undermined by your own sense of self-worth or you feel too vulnerable to throw off that bushel barrel that hides your light.

As I travel around the country speaking on topics ranging from "Overcoming Obstacles" to "Recovering from Breast Cancer" to "Making It as a Woman in a Male-Dominated Industry," I have become more and more convinced that understanding these seven truths is the key to our fulfillment as women, both personally and professionally. I am also convinced that women can best use their strengths without compromise in an entrepreneurial enterprise. But this book speaks to all women in a language that may seem foreign to most men and to most of the corporate world. Seeing these truths through the filter of love and courage is the fuel that drives the engine of our success—success on our own terms.

Part 2

three

Resiliency

P art of the natural ebb and flow of life is that things inevitably change and often go wrong. For as long as we're breathing, we will be challenged. Yet the quality of our lives is determined more by how we respond to changes and tough situations than the situations themselves. Our best responses come from our inner strengths—flexibility and resiliency.

We can all reflect upon changes and obstacles in our lives that woke up our creativity and turned into opportunities. The disruption of order in our lives is not only normal; it is the place from where breakthroughs come.

But we don't have to wait for a tragedy or an unexpected turn of events to discover our resilient spirit. We can be the victims of change or we can be the creators of it. But letting go of what's not working is a tough challenge.

We can fear challenges or we can face them head on and convert them into opportunities. We can become victims or take ownership of our own lives. Both men and women are capable of overcoming obstacles or making comebacks in their personal and business lives. Both can rise to the occasion but I contend that women are more likely to do so more successfully—and with a lot less complaining—because, among many other reasons, they are willing to take the road less traveled. Women approach this journey with courage and confidence because they are willing to reach out for help. (When was the last time you saw a man ask for directions when he was lost?) This openness to try new ways (or "thinking out of the box" to use one bit of contemporary business jargon) when combined with courage becomes a formula for resiliency. While men retreat to their "caves," as John Gray, Ph.D., author of *Men Are from Mars, Women Are from Venus*, puts it, women choose to engage their emotions. And provided women don't personalize the obstacles, their coping style gives them an advantage in many facets of life—including overcoming setbacks encountered in business.

Resiliency in Action

Congresswoman Carolyn McCarthy, wife, mother, and nurse of thirty years, represents much more than her constituents from Long Island, New York. She personifies resiliency and strength. She was thrust onto the public stage when a crazed gunman's random shots into a rush-hour commuter train killed her husband and injured her son.

Rather than allow this tragedy to defeat her, Carolyn McCarthy turned the incident into a public campaign against gun violence. "Women have so much power within themselves," she told me. "Something can really hurt and then as a typical woman, you get up the next morning and fight a little harder."

She went on to say that on her first day in Congress she was "scared stiff" but learned one day at a time how to do the job. I thought that was an interesting choice of adjective—"stiff"—being the opposite of flexible. She had been anything but stiff.

The week I visited with her she was involved in organizing the Million Mom March in Washington, D.C., to protest gun violence, proclaiming that women have always been on the forefront of social change in our country. According to Congresswoman McCarthy, women look for innovative ideas—simpler ways to make things happen. "When a woman says, 'Let's do it,' we get it done." Powerful words from a powerful lady—but then again, she says we all are. Some of us just don't know it—*yet*.

Congresswoman McCarthy's story makes several points about resiliency. First she didn't get stuck in her pain by personalizing it. It would seem to any reasonable person that life for her hasn't been fair. But while she undoubtedly entertained thoughts of unfairness, she chose not to stay there. Second, she engaged her emotions in a positive way. She felt her pain and channeled it into something in which she believed strongly. She chose to become a creator of change rather than a victim of it. And finally, she shares her passion for her chosen cause and, in turn, finds strength by reaching out to others.

Making Sense of the Senseless

Natural disasters strike innocent people. Destruction, disease, and other tragedies are indiscriminate. What happens doesn't happen *to* us; it just happens. When we stay stuck in "Why me?" we assume the role of victim, which renders us powerless to rise above it. When we become obsessed with trying to make sense of that which can't be reasoned, our intuition becomes suspended. We can't see the possibilities of the forced change. Healing is preempted by feelings of sadness and anger. Energy is replaced by fatigue and mental paralysis.

When I felt my life threatened by a potentially fatal disease, I was tempted to wallow in self-pity. I felt that I needed the answer to "Why me?" At that time, I reasoned that I should have been immune to breast cancer since I didn't smoke, I didn't drink, I was (and am) a health-conscious woman. I hadn't knowingly hurt anyone, so I argued that this tragedy couldn't possibly be a punishment. Why did it have to happen to me? And why now, at a time when so many others needed me?

Well, I still don't have the answers. I only know I'm thankful that I didn't stay there—stuck in that immobilizing internal dialogue. I learned that just because there are forces at play that are beyond my control, it doesn't mean I can't be the owner of my life—directing unpredictable change into something good. I learned to replace "Why me?" with "What now?" because "Why me?" makes us inactive. "What now?" empowers us to meet and greet the challenge.

The Power of Positive Language

Life's problems have great value. Problems make us strong. They build us up mentally. It's through facing the obstacles in life that we learn—about others and ourselves. And life's lessons tend to keep repeating themselves until we learn from them.

The force of our resilience is in direct proportion to our

positive perception of a particular situation. It's a matter of taking the power of positive thinking a step further. Positive language—the way we speak not only about the problem but also about the solution—can be a major factor in motivating us to action.

Once you've tapped into the courage to find the opportunities in a seemingly impossible situation, listen to how you talk about it. We've all used the phrases, "should have," "would have," "could have," which speak of regret. If I say that I *should* start my own company now that I've been laid off, I'm speaking at best passively about the idea. If I say that I am *going* to start my own company now that I've been laid off, I'm speaking actively about the idea. The same is true of "have." When I say to myself that I *have* to do something, it perpetuates my sense of dread, and doesn't help me to overcome inertia.

The subject of change reminds me of an encounter with a student who I met when I was lecturing at Texas A&M's College of Business in Corpus Christi. Carrie engaged me after the class to tell me how profoundly she was affected by the discussion about victim words and phrases and how in the face of setbacks, they zap our energy and creativity. She told me, "I constantly use victim words. I never realized how they were disconnecting me from my power to heal."

Carrie had been blindsided by the sudden end of her twenty-year marriage. She initially experienced it as a *personal* tragedy. Reluctantly, she had gone back to school to get a degree because she realized that she had limited skills and resources to make a living on her own.

Two years after our first meeting, I ran into Carrie at a university function. She confided that changing the way she talked about her life and her plans had made all the difference. In those two short years, she had completed her education and started a small tax service business. She had been able to change her perception of herself as a jilted divorcée who was forced to go back to school to a woman who now had an opportunity to pursue her unrealized potential.

Letting Go of What Isn't Working

For many women, our determination to persevere and to solve problems—to make a bad marriage work, for instance—will have us trying the same thing again and again, expecting to achieve a different result. It's impossible. Working harder or going faster in the wrong direction will not get you where you want to go. Yet, so many of us in the name of good intention resist change. In hopes of trying to maintain our happiness, we avoid problems. In doing so, we also avoid opportunities. Such is the strategy of a victim.

Just the other day, I talked to an intern at a Texas newspaper who told me flat out that she was not enjoying what she was doing. When I asked her what was preventing her from making a career change, she responded, "Journalism was my major, and I'm not a quitter." At twenty-two, Andrea has a lifetime to prove that she's no quitter! But somewhere, somehow, she got the message that persistence alone was the key to success and being a quitter was a bad thing. In effect, she had become a victim of her own misguided beliefs.

Unlike Andrea, I literally loved my job when I had to face a tough decision about quitting. I had been selling cars for two years when a management position in the finance department opened up. I believed that my sales experience and aptitude for numbers made me the perfect candidate for the job, so I asked for the promotion. My boss told me, "I can't spare you. You're my top gun in sales. It'd cost me—and you—money to promote you." I recall feeling hurt for a moment, thinking that maybe he really didn't think I'd cut it as a manager. Maybe he was trying to spare my feelings by calling me a "top gun." Whatever, his rejection was an obstacle in my career path, which I knew even then was to own my own business. That little voice inside me said that I couldn't make it to second base with one foot on first. Accepting that my fear of the unknown future was normal, I walked in the next morning with resignation in hand and determination in heart.

Do I regret my decision? What do you think?

What I did come to learn is that even though I was able to steer my career path in the direction I wanted (by seeking the confidence of another employer, I eventually landed a finance management position), in doing so, I accepted a new set of challenges. I was creating my own destiny with a conscious willingness to embrace the new problems that were sure to be a natural outcome of the change. And that willingness did wonders to enhance my self-esteem.

Don't Worry—Plan Instead

My dad once told me that he believes worrying must be a useful tool in life. When I asked him what he could possibly mean by such a statement, he replied: "Well, your mother is a worrier and hardly anything she ever worries about ever comes to pass. She must be heading it off!"

That's so true of worrying. The negative stuff we conjure up in our heads is a poor investment of time and energy because it rarely ever happens the way we imagine it. And worse, worrying about the future disturbs our peace of mind. It disconnects us from the present and jeopardizes our ability to think clearly. Worry creates pain and perpetuates a feeling of helplessness.

Planning is something different. Planning generates power and makes us feel secure. I have learned that if I'm prepared to meet a challenge, I'm able to approach it from a place of calm and intelligence.

In fact, not too long ago, I had an occasion to remind

myself about the power of planning. Feeling a bit anxious about a meeting with a couple of tough male colleagues scheduled for later in the day, I woke up at four A.M. with worry. To add to the challenge, one of the men was well known for his aggressive, almost bullylike communication style, and I'll say quite frankly, he had succeeded in intimidating me in the past.

At first, I played out all of the possible negative consequences in my mind. The "what if" scenarios seemed to multiply in my head. Unable to go back to sleep, I got up, made a cup of hot chocolate, lit a candle, and started writing my feelings down on paper. Feeling a little better, I next started cleaning out the refrigerator. It was either that or raid it.

That's when I realized that much of my anxiety was coming from the fact that I didn't have any idea how I would respond to any of the issues that were sure to come up in the course of the meeting. I wasn't even clear in my mind as to what I wanted the outcome to be. My thoughts had been so negative that I had no room to think clearly about the results I wanted to see.

With a new state of mind, I began to formulate a plan. One idea led to another. My self-perception changed from that of a woman in despair to a woman with a position. I went back to my pad and pen. In no time, I was eager to greet the day.

In the end, I used self-talk to reprogram my thinking. I was able to engage my brain to plan a strategy. My negative emotions gave way to facilitation of what turned out to be a very productive meeting—one I attended not as a victim but as a woman in control.

Finding Plan B

When we take charge of our destinies, it's important to remember that no matter how much we plan, life can still be unpredictable. The best-laid plans get derailed. And that's when it becomes especially important to stay focused on the big picture. That's because opportunities sometimes arrive on the scene when they're least expected and often in the form of a setback.

"Too often women get discouraged and say that they'll have to try again someday," says Barbara Robinson, CEO of STAR Associates and Self Pride, Inc. in Baltimore. She adds, "Your someday is now!" My observation is that the determination to be flexible is a common denominator in the life of every entrepreneur.

Sarian Bouma, an immigrant from Sierra Leone, says that in her pursuit of the "American dream," she had to remember that when one door closed she could always look for another marked ENTER.

Within a year of her arrival in the United States, she was enrolled in a community college *and* became a wife and mother. But before long, she found herself divorced with no steady income and a baby to support. She dropped out of college and in desperation turned to welfare and lived for a time in a women's shelter.

But Sarian was no victim. She applied for and managed to land an entry-level clerical position at a bank. In short order, she was promoted to customer service, where she spotted her "big opportunity." "I learned about the Small Business Administration and applied for a loan to start my own commercial cleaning service," she said, "Cleaning didn't require a large investment and I knew how to do it."

Today, Sarian owns a cleaning service, Capitol Hill Building Maintenance, Inc., which boasts 200 employees and annual revenues of $3.4 million!

Sarian stayed true to her conviction that she could have a good life if she was willing to keep trying. Though she was forced to deviate from her original course, she simply charted another.

Like Sarian, we can choose to activate our intuition and respond creatively. We can bounce back from adversity not simply to return to the same place at which it found us, but to rise above it.

An obstacle is the thing that stands between what you want and what you have. Sometimes the mountains we have to climb are treacherous, but it's on the journey that we learn most about ourselves. More often than not, it's only when we reach the top of the uphill climb that we are able to experience the beautiful rivers in the valleys of life.

four

Nurturing

E arly one morning a few months back, right smack in the
midst of a major project, my computer went on the blink.
I can type a blue streak, but when it comes to bits and bytes
my frustration level is in inverse proportion to my technical
skills. So I did what I've always done in a crisis. I called a
girlfriend. She empathized, telling me about a similar problem she'd had recently. Even though I was still staring at a
blank screen, after talking with her I felt that at the least I
wasn't the only computer-challenged woman in South Texas. I
hung up and dialed a computer-savvy colleague, who was

able to walk me briskly through a few troubleshooting hints to fix the problem. He might have been a little abrupt for my liking, but he got the job done and I found myself back at the keyboard in short order.

What both my girlfriend and my colleague were able to do for me in my minicrisis illustrates the essence of what I consider to be good business—solving a problem and making me, their customer as it were, feel better. Relying on just one or the other wasn't enough. Sure, I wanted the computer to do what's it's supposed to do, but I also didn't want to be left feeling like a complete idiot. I guess that's why I made the calls in the order I did.

So, at this point I'll unashamedly embrace the stereotype: Men, by their own admission, consider themselves to be "Mr. Fix-Its." They are, first and foremost, bottom-line problem-solvers. For them, getting to the destination is the point of setting out on the journey. Women, on the other hand, love to be helpful. Whether it's comforting a friend, nursing a child's skinned knee, helping raise funds for the symphony, or acting as a mediator in a meeting, a woman's inclination is to be a caretaker.

As an entrepreneur, my experience has shown that consumers need support, empathy, and guidance as well as solutions. They feel more comfortable when they're presented a menu of choices, not just a narrowly pitched resolution. And let's face it, not every consumer has a "problem." They may have only a desire that needs to be appreciated, an idea that needs to be expressed, or a dream that needs to be fulfilled . . . and a monkey wrench and a hammer alone aren't going to do the trick. This is where a woman's ability to nurture is a real asset. And when there is no readily discernable solution to be found, then the nurturing aspects of the relationship are essential.

I am not implying that women are completely selfless creatures with no concept of a bottom line. Nor am I suggesting that men are only driven by the profit motive. I am claiming that women and men tend to use different models. Women look to a model of support while men come at things with the intent to solve. These approaches should not, however, be mutually exclusive and, like the yin and yang of Chinese philosophy, the two should fit together to make a balanced, and profitable, whole.

Sarah, a young lady on my team, brings to her job as the finance manager a lifetime of nurturing. The oldest of five children of a single working mother, she accepted her role as a second parent. She continued to help support her family once she left school and joined my company. From day one on the job, she was always the first to volunteer to do more than her job description called for, to cover for other employees with personal and family issues, and to help new employees become part of our family.

Now, in her present job, she tackles some of the most delicate problems with understanding and sympathy. Talking money, reviewing a customer's credit history, negotiating financing that makes sense to both the company and the customer is pretty demanding for everyone involved. But by taking the time to listen and to understand that she is providing much more than financial counseling has made her highly successful at closing many different kinds of transactions.

Sometimes the result isn't exactly what one would anticipate but the benefits go far beyond simply closing the deal. In one recent case, an unemployed woman came in needing to buy a car but she didn't qualify for a loan. Rather than dismiss her as someone who couldn't purchase, Sarah understood that circumstances can change and even though she couldn't get past the potential customer's financial status, making a bond with this woman in trouble was important. A week later the lady returned with a family member who could and did buy a car. The woman praised Sarah because she had, in the customer's words, "been so loving." More referrals followed and several months later, the lady reapplied for a loan—this time with a brighter financial picture—and bought a brand-new car, thanks to Sarah.

Love and nurturing are rarely cited in a company manual or employee guidelines. They're certainly not part of the curriculum of any business school. But customers who feel that you care as much about them as you do about your business will be yours for life.

But nurturing a business involves much more than simply solving problems in a sympathetic way. There are many facets to nurturing, most of which are expressed in stereotypically feminine fashion: bonding, sharing, supporting, empathizing. By engaging any of these, the road to "closing the deal" becomes a richer and inevitably more rewarding experience both personally and financially for everyone involved.

Bonding

During the early part of the twentieth century, the American suffrage movement was coming into its full flowering. And although it took years of sweat and tears for women to get the vote and break down the many legal and social boundaries to equality, the unique bond that held women of every social and economic class together resulted in the most significant historical change of our time.

Committed women like Sojourner Truth, Mary Church Terrell, Ida B. Wells-Barnett, and Elizabeth Cady Stanton worked together to give all women a voice in their government. The suffragists organized and nurtured a sisterhood to engage in a peaceful movement that has endured as a foundation for all other women's rights.

Today, with the consumer clout that women possess, I believe that our willingness to reach out to one another—to befriend one another, not just make strategic alliances—gives us a real entrepreneurial advantage. An early selling experience of mine is a case in point. One sultry afternoon, the receptionist paged me to assist a mother and her teenage daughter who, as it turned out, had requested a female sales executive to help find a new car for the teenager. As I soon discovered, Dad, who hadn't come on this little shopping expedition, was not in favor of buying a car—at least not at that time. The mother asked me if I would accommodate her by working with them in a plan to persuade her husband to say yes to the new car.

The plan—okay, conspiracy—called for me to drive the car to their home that evening, which I did. Mom explained to Dad that I'd insisted that he should see the vehicle before making a final decision because everyone valued his opinion. During our conversation, the daughter went to sit in the new car while her mother took over the sales pitch. I didn't have to say much. You can imagine the rest of the story. Not only did I bond with mother and daughter, but Dad was convinced of my professionalism for insisting that he be consulted.

But sharing secrets and making plans aren't the only things that bind people together. Robert R. Provine, Ph.D., a professor of psychology and neuroscience at the University of Maryland, Baltimore County, concluded after ten years of study on the subject of laughter and humor that, "Laughter unites people, and social support has been shown in studies to improve mental and physical health. Indeed, the presumed health benefits of laughter may be coincidental consequences of its primary goal: bringing people together." And in a similar case study, it was concluded that females laugh more than men do. It's no surprise. Women enjoy laughing. Pick up any publication that runs matchmaker ads. Women are much more likely than men to seek out a mate with a "sense of humor."

Mutual laughter is very nurturing. No relationship can survive well without it. Humor is the glue that holds many a family and business together and helps one through some awkward situations.

I recall one time at a board meeting I made a recommendation absent any forethought. I barely got it out of my mouth when the other board members started blurting out criticisms of it. I felt myself get flushed as they fell all over each other to declare what a dumb idea I had proposed. When they finally stopped talking, I looked around the table at all of them and said, "Hey, you've got to give me credit. I was thinking outside of the box." They laughed and I rebounded back to a place of respect. Of course, being able to laugh at yourself takes a lot of confidence, but that's another story for another chapter.

I know that any time I hear a customer laughing in an office with a salesperson, a transaction is more than likely in progress. A connection is being made. When people are laughing together, it's like they're sharing a moment. They're attached to each other by the same reaction to an external stimulation.

I dare say that having a sense of humor is as important in

business as having common sense. Engaging with someone in a cause or sharing a moment of humor creates an environment for sharing. And ladies, that's a game we've learned well.

Sharing

As young girls, we were programmed to share. We heard, "It's nice. People will like you." We're still doing it and I believe it's a good thing. I've heard it said that one of the reasons women don't get ahead or aren't further along in the business world is because we don't help each other. Let's stop blaming—blaming men and blaming each other. While I'm sure there are some exceptions, most women rising to the top are sharing—their resources and their experiences.

Working Woman magazine is the driving force behind the annual Top 500 Women-Owned Businesses in America list. In addition, each year the magazine hosts a unique summit for women business leaders and those aspiring female entrepreneurs who want to learn from them. Businesses across the board are represented, from trucking to technology, makeup to media—and yes, even automotive. The event also provides female entrepreneurs access to information on digital business, diversity, partnerships, e-commerce, global trade, and, best of all, each other. It's an opportunity to re-create the "old boys' network" without the exclusivity. And it represents a movement across the country that brings women together in the spirit of sharing rather than competition.

Taking this spirit into the digital age is twenty-something Aliza Pilar Sherman, one of *Newsweek*'s Top 50 People Who Matter Most on the Internet, who didn't just join the dot-com gold rush, but in fact helped pioneer it. A believer in the power of the Internet to create and accelerate opportunities for women, she co-founded Cybergrrl, Inc. and Webgrrls International in 1995. For the first time in the history of computer technology, there was a website and Internet organization providing a forum for female entrepreneurs. An on-line community that offered women inspiration, access, advice, and the tools to make their dreams come true now existed.

But Aliza went one step further. Of Mexican descent, she decided to combine her professional passion with her personal heritage by building the first bilingual online network for Latinas, EVIVA.NET. Feeling that Hispanic women were an underserved yet potent economic force, she harnessed the buying power and entrepreneurial spirit of some 600,000 Latinas running small businesses. She took notice that Hispanic women often control the purse strings in their families and considering there's $350 billion in those purses, EVIVA.NET is a remarkable property. Her creation gave new meaning to networking—girl talk for the new millennium.

The women at *Working Woman* magazine and Aliza have directed their life's work toward sharing. They're women who make their living helping other women. They've used their nurturing side to create and provide a community where women can nurture one another to health and wealth.

The Art of Closing the Deal

In business, as much as we should enjoy the journey that building relationships provides, there is still the bottom line—making the sale, closing the deal.

Closing involves a transaction. And for a transaction to take place, at least two people have to be engaged in a relationship. All relationships are at their best when they've been nurtured. For parties to come to terms, each must feel that the benefit or value is equal to or greater than what's being relinquished. It amounts to a trade. And if you think about it, relationships are also trades. The principle of "give and take" is involved in every transaction and every relationship.

From my perspective as a woman who has something of a reputation as a "closer," it seems that we've been using the wrong term all together. If you close a door, you shut others out. If you close a store down it means the end of business. The closing of a business transaction is but one step along the road. After the close, life goes on and it should go on better than before—for everyone.

Closing is not the art of twisting—arms, minds, or words. And it doesn't involve being pushy. No woman wants to be thought of as a "pushy broad" after all. In fact, a close should be anticlimactic—as inevitable to a transaction as a period is to the end of this sentence. A closing is really a beginning.

In my sales career, I have many times been referred to as a good closer. I recall that once my closing abilities were even referred to as being "lethal." What was that supposed to mean? I suppose it was a guy's way of saying that I was highly effective at escorting customers from "Hi. How may I be of assistance?" to "Thanks for your business." Yet I cannot recall ever thinking during the process that I was going in for the close, let alone the kill. I simply did what came naturally. By the time I was discussing terms with a customer, we were friends. We had established a relationship.

In every healthy relationship, offerings are made that have the welfare of both parties in mind. I know that my car dealerships serve to improve the quality of people's lives—my own included. That's okay, because in the end I know that I work hard to live up to my end of the bargain, which includes offering my customers a full opportunity to purchase the products and services that I sell. Therefore, if you truly believe it's in the customer's best interest to do business with you, it's your duty to present the offering—otherwise known as the closing. If you forget about this part of the transaction you are effectively denying your customer an opportunity. And if you don't think of a close as a service that you owe your customer, go back and reexamine your motives for being in business.

A woman I know who practices this I-owe-it-to-them philosophy tells a funny story about one of her so-called closing experiences. Georgiana is a businesswoman who is passionate about her ability to help other business people and she does so by creating and developing radio-advertising packages for them. Her specialty is small businesses with limited advertising budgets.

One prospective client, an owner of a small chain of bakeries, had never advertised on the radio before so Georgiana created "from scratch" a sample commercial for his consideration, promoting his "made from scratch" holiday pies. She then scheduled and reserved the time for the commercials to air when working moms would most likely hear them—the time when they would be driving to or from work.

Given that there were only ten shopping days remaining until Christmas, she accomplished all of this within a short time and on the bakery owner's tentative budget, which was a subject that had only been touched upon. She then drew up the agreement and headed over to the bakery owner's office to close the deal. Normally she did this in a way that was enlightening to her clients and helped them become better informed about the world of advertising. But less than halfway through her price presentation to the bakery owner, he interrupted her and said, "What is this? I'm already closed!"

She never even got to the point where she would typically ask, "Are you comfortable with what this plan can do for you and your business?" or "Am I safe in assuming that this plan meets your business objectives?"—great closing questions, by the way.

But Georgiana didn't need them because she put herself in the shoes of her client, focusing her attention on the benefit of the transaction to *his* business, not hers. I believe her story paints a great portrait of what a close is supposed to look like in a business deal. When a customer's needs are the centerpiece of a negotiation and nurtured up front, a good close is inevitable.

This perspective on closing certainly doesn't fit with the sharklike reputation with which so many sales transactions are burdened. But there's no better way I can think of to grow your business than to nurture your customers. Finding out what they want is the first step. Finding out a way to make it happen is the next. Upon reflection, I wear my title of "good closer" with pride.

Support, Empathy, and Truth

As human beings, we feel connected to someone who supports us in our mission. We feel safe with someone who feels our pain. And we feel trusting of someone who tells us the truth. Each of these concepts is part of a three-step process that I see as nurturing in action. And while this process is inherently part of every interaction, it's particularly important to recognize and reinforce these steps when dealing with a difficult situation.

Whenever you need to calm someone down in hopes of getting through to him or her, think of the acronym SET. Here's how it works: We all know that when a person is upset, they're not thinking clearly and when someone's not thinking clearly, they're not apt to process logical truths. They're in a world where they need to feel, first and foremost, supported. That's what the S stands for. The first statement made to them has to be one of support. Once you've done that, follow up with a showing or telling of empathy; hence, the E. Next, the truth can be told (the T), but only after support and empathy are conveyed.

My first experience applying the SET technique was with a man who was in a tirade in the showroom demanding to see the "woman boss." This out-of-control character was yelling at the top of his voice. His face was so red I thought he might be on the verge of having a heart attack.

Totally unaware of what his issues were, by some grace, I remembered the SET strategy. As I approached him, he started rambling about how someone in the service department had not fixed his car right. Remaining as calm as I could, I impressed upon him that I understood how important it was for him to get his car fixed, and fixed right. Once he recognized that I supported him, he calmed down somewhat and I was able to tell him that I recognized how much this matter was really bothering him (empathy). He calmed down more. Finally, I was able to ask him to come into my office where we could access his records. I know in my heart that if I had demanded he come into my office straightaway, he'd probably have told me what I could do with his file.

Like closing a deal, working through a difficult encounter like this one meant using all my feminine strengths—compassion, empathy, understanding—rather than brute strength to heave the guy out of my showroom. We did solve his problem and he left with his car fixed and his dignity intact.

Self-Nurturing

For most women, nurturing is second nature and they can use this special talent in their business lives to great advantage. But all too often, they forget to nurture themselves. Self-nurturing is essential for preventing that business killer called "burnout."

According to the Hilton Time Values Project, 26 percent of those surveyed considered themselves to be workaholics. And while the focus of many of these studies may have been on men, it's not hard to imagine that women—who are trying to make their way in the business world while still being the main keepers of the home—will be as susceptible to burnout as men are. Personally, I've seen more than one of my employees go up in flames. But I must confess that while I've learned the importance of self-nurturing, I'm still learning the art.

Margo Provost is a lady who learned a great lesson about self-love and then went on to create a business sharing what she learned. She spent the first three years of her life in an orphanage before she was adopted. The only problem was that her new family setting wasn't exactly of the storybook variety. She felt at times unloved and unlovable. She learned to cope and befriend herself by journaling in her diary.

When she was of legal age to leave home, she enrolled in a state university with a student loan and two jobs to pay her way, eventually earning degrees in Nutrition and Physiological Biochemistry.

Then in her twenties, living alone, she set out to apply her education and life lessons by creating a plan to build a nurturing haven where people could come and find physical and spiritual nourishment.

Log Haven, located on forty beautiful acres in Utah, is the result of Margo's self-nurturing drive. It houses one of Utah's Ten Most Popular Restaurants and serves as a refuge for people in need of tender, loving care. She also finally dismissed the notion that she was "unlovable" and married a man she describes as wonderful.

The message in Margo's story is that the first person you have to take care of is yourself. She used a self-nurturing strategy to survive tough times. Taking care of her needs by listening to herself and looking ahead, she designed a business and a life she loves.

Maybe your needs are somewhat less severe than Margo's were. In the end, it usually doesn't take much to pay yourself a little attention. Karen Zelina, owner of Questlink in San Jose, California, says that she schedules "time to think" everyday. She closes her office door and the eighty employees of the company respect her practice, knowing that an interruption is out of the question. Because she first honors her solitude, they do too. She emerges fresher to respond to their needs because she doesn't ignore one of hers—the need for solitude.

In our effort to be superwomen, we tend to fill every minute of every day with some kind of something. When we turn the page of a calendar, it looks like it's been to war. It's no wonder we suffer from battle fatigue. I've learned to schedule Marion-only days. Some days I tackle a closet. Some days I just hang out in my favorite bathrobe. When I'm running on fumes and I see a heavenly blank spot up ahead, it's like I'm able to give my project, whatever it is, that final kick. And when I've totally indulged myself with a blank day—I'm shooting for a week—I return to the front with less resentment and more pep than I would have otherwise.

When we tend to our own needs, we're better able to tend to others. Even on planes, the flight attendant's announcement calls for those traveling with small children to place the oxygen mask on themselves before they place one on the child. Practice the same concept in business and you'll see how much more logic prevails. Keeping the flame of your passion alive means taking recesses to take care of your best friend—you!

Women bring a real strength to the business table: their let-me-take-care-of-you approach. In our fast-paced, fast-fast techno business culture, it's a welcome trait. I've heard futurists say that we've got to be prepared to surprise our customers with new, innovative gadgets. How about surprising them with great service?

Bonding with other people to further a cause comes naturally for women. The giggling schoolgirl evolves into a woman who recognizes that her willingness to laugh at herself and tough times is an asset. It unites people, whether it's a twosome or a whole roomful.

Born (or made) people-pleasers, women are holding their hands up for other women. They're sharing everything from their microphones to their mistakes. And I believe that when women become comfortable sharing how-to-buy information in a not-so-shy way with their customers, they're sure to improve the quality of life for all involved.

Nurturing is a way of life for most women and I have learned that even the toughest of situations and people in business respond favorably to a showing of support and empathy. A sometimes harsh truth lands easier on a person when they've first been nurtured. My business slogan is "Love keeps you going." An eye on the bottom line is always important in business but for a business to enjoy healthy growth and longevity, strategic planning is best replaced with supportive planning. In the end, if you're supporting your market by providing them with creative ideas and surprising service, your strategy meetings will become celebrations!

Nurturing is about building relationships—with your customers, your colleagues, your peers, your competitors, your community. But it is also about creating results. Whether you nurture children to a happy and healthy adulthood, sustain a marriage through good and bad times to contented old age, or bring a garden to full flowering, in the end there will be results of which you can be proud.

Other typically female strengths complement a willingness and ability to care for others. By tapping into your keen sense of what you see and hear, putting your intuitive nature to work for you, you'll find yourself creating new and better ways of nurturing your business.

five

Intuition

The way we women lay claim to intuition, you'd think it's as exclusive to our gender as childbearing. After all, who ever heard of "masculine intuition"? Since I've already confessed to being something of a pragmatist, I feel compelled to scrutinize this mystical thing called intuition. I don't believe it's some magical trait exclusive to women, but historically women have been able to express their intuitive side in a way that most men have not. Most important, I do think that intuition is grossly misunderstood.

I was riding home from a big wedding reception listening

to my date give me this I-want-some-of-what-you've-got spiel, saying that he thought that I was "gifted" at connecting with people.

"There's no secret to it," I confessed. "Connecting starts with noticing." We then started playing a little game in which each of us made a list of all of the observations we had made of people at the reception. My list was so long that I didn't know where to stop. He didn't know where to start. With some prompting he recalled a few details about what people wore, who was sitting next to whom, or who seemed to be having a good time but, as I've long suspected, he just proved my theory that there is an "observation gap" between men and women. That night ours had been as wide as the Grand Canyon. He hadn't even noticed that the best man had spinach in his teeth for half the night!

I recall that encounter whenever I am asked to define intuition because "seeing" is the first sense to come into play in this extrasensory trait of intuition. I'd like to take intuition out of the realm of the paranormal by demonstrating that intuition is, in fact, the art of reading signals and recognizing patterns. But seeing and observing are only two steps in the intuitive process. When seeing and observing become awareness, then the process is complete. Intuition is like any talent: If you don't practice and use it, it will disappear. Intuition is made active, and becomes a powerful tool in business, when awareness is deepened by asking questions and listening to those answers.

The power of intuition lies primarily in its ability to predict human behavior, if not for actually foretelling the future. And whether your aim is to please your mother-in-law, figure out what's bothering your teenager, or come up with a strategic plan for your business, acknowledging and developing intuition is invaluable.

Just ask Faith Popcorn, the author whose name is synonymous with forecasting. She's been predicting business trends with remarkable accuracy for the past two decades. Business leaders consume her prophecies as if they came from the Bible.

And then there's Martha Stewart. She sold us a complete lifestyle before we even knew what it was we wanted. She tapped into the dormant creative homemaking spirit in millions of women. So what if we didn't have a staff of twelve to help us decorate, cook, and garden up to Ms. Stewart's standards. She showed us the dream, and then franchised it at your nearest discount department store.

Oprah Winfrey, considered to be one of the most powerful women in the world, uses her extraordinary ability to trend-spot to bring women what they want. I bought a pair of after-sport shoes recently just because Oprah said she wears them and never wants to take them off. Her power of endorsement is a tribute to the trust women place in her. It's like we look at her as a life guide. She's out there "noticing" things for our own good.

These women don't claim to be clairvoyant but you can bet

they wouldn't be where they are today if they didn't engage in reading the signals and recognizing the patterns.

Debi Davis is another entrepreneur, perhaps not quite so legendary as Popcorn, Stewart, or Winfrey, but equally adept at activating intuition. Ten years ago, her life was out of control. A newly divorced mother of two small children, Debi was physically, financially, and personally distressed. With no particular skills and limited education, she needed to provide for her children and get her life back together. And so she created Kidsport Jr. Gym, an unlikely venture for a woman with limited business experience and whose 210 pounds on her small frame weren't exactly ideal for an exercise leotard. But her new venture gave her the flexibility to generate an income and care for her own children.

At the same time, fighting to regain her self-esteem, she embarked on a successful weight-loss program, and it wasn't long before the moms coming to her kid's gym were asking for her "secret." That motivated her to hock her Rolex watch, her only valuable possession, and publish a booklet on her weightloss program, hence giving birth to another small business.

Today her "small" business, Fit America Inc., is a $48 million retail franchise operation with more than seventy stores nationwide specializing in weight-loss herbal products. Honed by necessity, she saw the signals and recognized the patterns—overweight women wanting to get help and a growing acceptance of alternative remedies in the health market.

As with so many women entrepreneurs, she measures her success in both personal and financial terms. Today, she's a healthy 128 pounds and has reclaimed her watch (which she now wears with added diamonds), as a timeless reminder that she's not only reclaimed her life, she has made it even better.

Reading Signals

How many times has your husband, boyfriend, or other man asked you how you could tell that someone was mad, or sad, or glad when he saw no clues? It almost seems that women have special antennae that allow them to transcend distracting sights and sounds.

When it comes to insight, men claim—sometimes even boast—to have laserlike focus. While this may be generally true, it comes at a cost. They miss a lot of small and important details. Women, on the other hand, seem to have the ability to pick up information off the screen by using their peripheral vision. One theory is that this gender difference is evolutionary. Men, the hunters, had to set their sights on the target and stay fixed. Women, the gatherers, had to look all around to find just the right berries. In any event, their peripheral vision helps women to see things many men miss.

I have firsthand experience to know that gathering important information means sometimes looking beneath the surface. From my stint as a finance manager, I recall a couple who became evasive when I asked them a routine question for their credit application. (It was something like "What are your Social Security numbers?") At first I felt like I was talking to a blank wall. Did they think they were above having to go through this inquiry?

Then the writing began to appear on that blank wall. The wife became fidgety. The husband kept wiping his hands on his pant legs. They weren't only evasive. They were nervous. Without playing amateur psychologist, I wondered if something I said had embarrassed them. I walked behind them and closed the door. As I returned to my side of the desk, I touched the wife on the shoulder. I sat down, took a deep breath, and started explaining to them that many of the customers I talked with in the course of my work had credit "snags" of some kind. Seldom, I continued, was there a situation for which we couldn't find a solution. The conversation flowed from there.

I learned that their daughter's illness had set them back financially two years earlier. (Little did they know with whom they were sharing their story!) They knew that their bad credit history was about to be revealed and even though they realized it was unavoidable, it didn't make the ordeal any easier for them. The signals of what was really going on in the minds of this couple were clear. They just weren't *loud and clear*—at least not at first anyway.

Seeing and Observing

Recently, I had occasion to talk about women's intuition with renowned psychologist Dr. Joy Browne. She said that because women are better at reading body language they have the makings to be better salesmen than most men she knows.

If you're like me, you've purchased and read the body language books, but reading body language is much more than just looking at the way someone's arms are crossed or the way they're holding their fingers. It's important to be attentive to the subtle nuances, the way someone turns down the corners of their mouth, or the way they release a small sigh, or the way they shift their weight in their chair.

It's also interesting to recognize that when a man and a woman act out the very same body movement it does not necessarily mean the same thing. For example, a woman shifting from side to side in her chair or otherwise acting antsy (like the woman with the bad credit rating) is probably nervous. A man behaving that way might simply be bored. But anyone honing her body language skills will also be on the alert for staged performances. If a body statement is exaggerated— like someone sitting at a sharp ninety degree angle or someone piercing you with deliberate, unblinking eye contact, chances are their body language is a mask for a hidden feeling or attitude.

Hearing and Listening

So far what I've emphasized is the visual aspect of reading signals. But what about the audio? Do women hear better than men? Medically speaking, there's probably no difference but there certainly is an argument to make about how women listen in a different (better?) way than men do. Men have a tendency to listen only for the "meat" of what's being said. One of my male competitor's former employees told me that his ex-boss's favorite saying is "Spare me the labor. Give me the baby." That might be a crude way of putting it, but I believe this is typical of the way most men gather information. (Remember the story of the hunter compared with the gatherer?)

When I was selling cars, I was expected to (and I would) take the information I had gathered from my customer to my sales manager. He would typically be in his office positioned to "advise" the sales reps as to how to proceed with their sales transactions. In making my presentation, it amazed me how many times I'd be interrupted with a comment like, "Just give me the bottom line." To me, coming in there with only the "bottom line" was like offering someone a punch line with no joke. How could he really be equipped to guide me with so little information? Working in a male-dominated field has taught me that men definitely hear fewer words in a conversation than women do. That's the way they seem to prefer it.

And while men tune out seemingly trivial comments, women process them for potentially important clues. The same remark a man finds to be useless, a woman might judge to be meaningful. One male executive of an international Fortune 500 company confessed that he chose to ignore his wife when she warned him to watch his back with a newly hired manager.

She heard an alarm go off when the new manager proclaimed at dinner one evening that business was "like love and war." Her husband could barely even recall the remark. She was eventually proven to be right when the overly ambitious manager underhandedly usurped his boss's authority— and position. The husband learned the hard way to listen, if not like his wife, at least to his wife.

Women don't just listen to what is said but how it's said. When an angry man tells his wife that everything's "just fine!" she knows not to take him literally. His "fine" means "Don't bug me," or maybe even "Come baby me," but it doesn't mean that all is well. Perhaps the idea that women will read between the lines means that they have the courage to look deeper into the circumstances and accept whatever they find there. But that's another story.

Women listen to what's said with their ears *and* hearts. Being the emotional creatures that we are, we know that emotions are revealed through inflection, volume, and tone. It is peripheral listening that reveals the true meaning behind any statement.

Like bodies, voices speak many languages of attitude and

agenda. A person who mumbles is probably unsure of themselves. A person who ends every sentence with a turned-up word—virtually turning a suggestion into a question—is looking for approval.

Being attentive to the emotion of sound is wise. Along with peripheral vision, reading body language and listening to everything that is spoken and unspoken allows us to read all the signals.

Recognizing Patterns

I was impressed by a local weatherman's report the other night that predicted weather patterns that would have a significant impact on my region of South Texas. The weather is not unlike human behavior and trying to predict either can be a challenge. But using the most sophisticated monitoring equipment and their own experience, most professionals can do a pretty good job on either. Instead of the Doppler 2000 or some other space-age device favored by the weather service, most people need to rely on finely honed intuition to anticipate the behavior of others. While there will always be the unexpected storm, it's safe to assume that when x conditions are present, then y happens. That is, if we've read the signals and recognized the patterns.

I never thought of myself as a trend spotter. But after sharing many stories with other women entrepreneurs, I realize that I based my entire business model on an observed behavioral pattern. In my case, it was a pattern of neglect. From my days as a receptionist in a car dealership, time and again I witnessed women being ignored in the showrooms. Although it wasn't until circumstances forced me to look for work that I was convinced of the need and the potential for success of a female car dealer.

I knew that women drove cars. I knew that women had at least some say-so in buying cars. And I had also observed that not many women were selling them. (Of course, I didn't know then what I know now, that women make up only 7.7 percent of the nation's total sales force at car dealerships!)

I know that much of my success is due to the fact that I catered to both halves of couples as well as the flurry of single and divorced women visiting car dealerships in a state of dread and apprehension. Early on, many men in this business missed this trend. But you can bet that my intuition influences every element of every business decision I make.

I've learned to look for other patterns too. Because today's consumers are fickle by nature, I look at patterns of buyer behavior with intense interest. For example, I track how consumers respond to particular types of advertising. (There are expensive marketing studies out there, but they're effectively using the same tool that I do—looking for patterns.) I track what radio station customers' trade-ins are tuned to. If I'm spending money with a radio station other than the one to which my customers are primarily listening, I can conclude that my advertising dollars are not working efficiently.

In fact, I plot so many patterns in my businesses and hold meetings with so many charts and graphs that I've been asked if I'm kin to Ross Perot (remember that men use these techniques too).

But passive intuition, even if you understand how it works, needs to be turned into a power tool. Plug it in by simply exercising your natural curiosity.

Asking the Right Questions

I think that women are, by nature, more curious than men are. Perhaps we are simply unafraid to ask questions or we don't let our egos get in the way of getting the information we want and need. At the risk of making a sweeping generalization, allow me to make reference to that old stereotype about men who would rather wander aimlessly than ask for directions or suffer through a Christmas Eve trying to assemble little Becky's playhouse without reading the directions.

Mastering the art of asking questions is something for which women are primed. But I also believe that curiosity is a trait common to entrepreneurs of both sexes.

Marc Anthony, a popular Latin artist, sings a song, "I

Need to Know," that could serve as an anthem for all entrepreneurs. I need to know if I can do it. I need to know if it's possible. I need to know if there's a better way. I need to know what customers want. It's this kind of curiosity that leads to learning. And learning leads to knowing.

Picking up clues from signals and patterns is one way to get the scoop but unless you're a mind reader, you're going to be like the mathematician trying to solve an equation with too many variables. To learn everything you need to know, there is no shortcut or detour. You've got to ask the right questions. But even that's not enough. You've got to listen to the answers.

I am reminded of Carolyn, a residential realtor who is "by nature" an inquisitive person, so asking questions for her comes fairly easy. She says that whenever she's showing a property, she'll typically ask the couple, "Who does the yard work?"

The answers range from, "She's the one with the green thumb," to "We'll need to save room in the budget for a gardener," to "We don't need a big lot—neither one of us likes yard work."

Imagine Carolyn's reaction one day when she posed that question to a couple and the woman responded, "His gay partner will." At this point, she wasn't even certain who the client was.

Her sensitive response was—you got it—another question. "When may I show him the property?" At this point, it was like opening up an information floodgate. The couple present were a brother and a sister. The sister was going to be renting a room from the brother and his partner. And so on and so on.

Carolyn learned by asking questions—not only what the customers needed but also who the customers were. Both sides got to know each other better. In business, probing (delicately) for information is the part of the communication where both parties are actually doing the same thing together—defining the need and determining the solution. You'll know you're on the right track when you hear your customer (or partner, employee, or other associate for that matter) saying things like, "Oh, good question. I haven't thought about that," or "Gosh, I haven't given that any consideration."

On a recent television biography of Barbara Walters, I was impressed by how many of her peers were so respectful of her interviewing style. Many journalists, highly respected in their own right, presented their insider perspectives on her career and I couldn't help but take away from the program a couple of well-made points about the art of asking questions.

Of course, Walters is envied for landing the most coveted interviews. When asked why he agreed to be interviewed by her, one famous subject cited a trust factor. He felt that she would be fair and wouldn't "go for the jugular." Another point that resonated from the testimonies was that she's a master at "timing" her questions. One of her colleagues called it "skillful pacing."

No matter what the situation, trust is the most important link between two people. If a client or colleague is mistrustful of you, you're not very well positioned to seek information from them. If you've hurt someone in the past with their own revelations, why would they want to return for seconds? When you're asking a customer questions, it's important to let them know that you're asking for the purpose of helping them. (It amazes me how often I've witnessed this simple step skipped over all together.)

Have you ever heard any interviewer ask the most important question first? I suppose if there was such a course as Question Asking 101, the most basic principle taught would be what entertainers refer to as "pre-heating" an audience. The name of the concept speaks for itself. I won't elaborate except to stress that the same tip can be applied in business. For many fast-moving entrepreneurs who have a direct style of communication this is a tough idea to follow.

Barbara Walters–type timing may be a tribute to a special instinct she possesses. I won't debate that. I won't even suggest that any of us can duplicate her style. But I can promise you, she uses a watchful eye and a keen sense of listening to pick up nuances during the course of her interviews. She also complements her abilities with hard work. She does her research so that she is aware of past behavior. Like a good lawyer, she rarely asks a question to which she probably doesn't already know the answer—or when she isn't pretty sure she's on the right track. Then and only then does she ask her chosen question.

Occasionally, we encounter someone who is very reserved and even withholding. It's almost like we're being stonewalled. Getting past this block can be frustrating but I've discovered more than one way to make a breakthrough. But one effective technique I've seen comes with a warning: It should not be overused. By repeating a key phrase during the course of your conversation, you can ask the other person to explain or elaborate without a direct question. Well-trained psychiatrists are masters of this technique but it's actually a communication skill anyone can use.

I experimented with this tool by asking five girlfriends to use it. The following are some of the results.

Husband:	I forgot your birthday.
Wife:	Forgot?
Husband:	Well, I really didn't forget. I called you early this morning but couldn't reach you. Not even the recorder was on.

Client:	A priority for me is security.
Real Estate Agent:	Security?
Client:	I won't live in a subdivision that isn't gated.

Employer:	I need logical data.
Employee:	Logical data?

Employer: Last week in your report all I read
              were opinions. This time try to focus
              on specifics backed by statistics.

Remember the caution: Don't overuse this tool. Obviously, if this is the only form of communication you use, you're going to begin to sound like a trained parrot. But it is a way to listen to what's unspoken and invite the speaker to give you more.

Providing consumers with what they want and need should be on every entrepreneur's agenda for success. No one opens up a business and says; "I don't care what pleases customers. I refuse to let them push me around." We do care what pleases customers. But in reality, we don't want to be pushed around. We prefer to draw our customers toward solutions that will amaze them. This requires forward thinking and forward thinking requires knowledge of the present and the past. Intuition is fully activated by asking all the right questions and then—listening.

Listening and Learning

You can't possibly inform or persuade people unless you can engage them first. And to keep them interested, you have to be able to hear not only what they're saying but also what they're thinking. You have to be able to hear not only their spoken but also their unspoken responses. In the end, you'll be better able to detect potential problems and plan for solutions.

I got one of my most important lessons in listening from an all-boys' club. I once served on a commission for which I was the first woman member in the club's seventy-year history. My peers were six well-respected businessmen.

One of those men was probably the quietest person I've ever known. He sat next to me at the commission meetings and as we opened up our notebooks to begin the meeting, I couldn't help but notice that his material was highlighted, paper-clipped, and dog-eared. He had clearly done more than peruse the documents. Yet, his comments at the meetings were rare. At one point, I remember thinking, "He's not going to make it on this board. He's too quiet."

I, on the other hand, made certain that I had a comment or a question related to every agenda item. I felt a tremendous responsibility to my gender, being the first woman on that board. I didn't want the men ever to be able to say, "We had a woman on this board—once." I truly thought that having a loud voice meant having a strong voice. Yet, there were times I felt like my eloquence was being received like the sound of scratches across a chalkboard, but I didn't listen. I didn't listen to my well-meaning critics and I didn't listen to my inner voice—at least for a while.

Then I began to pay closer attention to my quiet colleague. I noticed that when the chairman called on him to respond, his comments were profound and succinct. Right before he began to speak, he would take a deep breath and look up at the ceiling as though he was receiving his words from some higher authority. The room was so quiet you could hear a pin drop. Everyone (sometimes hundreds) in the room was waiting with bated breath to hear what he had to say.

I later nicknamed him E. F. Hutton. Remember the commercial? "When E. F. Hutton talks, people listen." That was my colleague all right. His listening style armed him with great information. He went on to become the chairman of the commission and I, much to my lasting humiliation, was ousted!

I think of listening as the other side of asking questions. In fact, there's a lot less need for asking questions when we do a good job of listening. But too often we're too busy thinking about what we're going to say next. One clue that you could improve your listening skills is if you don't remember people's names. Or, do you look for places in people's conversations to slide in with a quip or a joke or even worse an argument? Listening should be easy and yet for so many of us, it's so hard. Just like the art of asking questions, good listening may require us to check our egos at the door. (And need I say, that for women this may be a lot easier a task than for men?)

We've all heard the jokes about psychiatrists who charge big bucks to sit there and say nothing. They draw people out of themselves with short questions (recall the technique of repeating a key phrase) but for the most part, silence is their most potent weapon. Nature abhors a vacuum and people have this insatiable need to fill silence with words. Let them.

Doctors are one professional group whose master of active listening is critical. Their patients are their customers and the diagnosis is the equivalent of assessing their needs.

My own physician talks of one of the challenges of her profession. In a very short amount of time, she's got to build a rapport with her patient in order to make the best diagnosis. She uses that time not only for a physical examination but also to ask questions. She listens to their responses very closely for subtle or hidden messages that might be of value.

She begins each session by reading the patient's chart, usually right outside the door of the examination room where she can hear the patient stirring. Then she walks in, makes eye contact, and offers a friendly introduction. She remains standing because she feels she is more attentive. Before she asks a specific question about symptoms, she offers a positive comment about something on the chart. It might be something along the lines of "I see you've been successful in losing eight pounds since your last visit" or "I see you work at my favorite restaurant."

Even though her time is precious, she gains a lot from asking a benign question. The patient has an opportunity to relax and the doctor establishes rapport, which is the first step toward building trust. Her experience has shown her that this small gesture of interest dissolves, or at least diminishes, a patient's inhibitions, giving her more access to more information. "It's not easy," she says. "I probe in more ways than one and I have to listen actively instead of passively." That's the trick for all of us. Are you simply hearing or are you really listening?

As women, we're likely to think we have a monopoly on intuition. We don't. And while we may be predisposed toward having it, in truth, like any other talent, it's got to be developed to be useful. It's a human resource that has countless business applications.

In this climate of constant change, forecasting can head off a potential disaster or create an environment for opportunity. Consumers have come to expect change in the way of new products and innovative ways of doing things. This responsibility has fallen on the shoulders of today's entrepreneurs. Yet with change comes risk. To minimize risks we need information. In business, where it's no longer good enough to satisfy customers, having access to meaningful data is not a luxury. Today's consumers are telling us loud and clear, "I don't want you to meet my expectations. I want you to give me a serving of the unexpected. I want you to surprise me."

Our finely tuned active intuition links us to create new ways of doing things and new products. And like intuition, women are inclined toward creativity. These two traits have not often enough been emphasized in business books and courses for entrepreneurs—until now.

six

Creativity

Creativity is an offspring of intuition. While intuition involves picking up signals and recognizing patterns, creativity gives birth to a new order. And like its parent, intuition, creativity is greatly misunderstood. While it's true our world has known many creative geniuses, there is no such thing as a gifted few. All of us (men and women) have at least some small portion of this so-called gift, and like intuition, it needs to be cultivated to bear fruit.

To make a difference, you must be different. The "me

too" mentality does not fit the entrepreneur. And it surely doesn't fit the woman trying to make her way in the world of business. As women, we may stake claim to being problem-solvers, but it takes creativity to solve problems. And it takes some ingenuity to live your life actively instead of passively. Yet, at the same time, we have to be prepared for the results of our own creativity that may threaten our secure and predictable world.

Sometimes discovering your creative self means letting go of your "tears and fears," or so says entrepreneur and consultant Linda Novey-White. While recovering from surgery for uterine cancer and undergoing chemotherapy—and being newly separated from her husband—Linda had to come up with a plan to bring in some money—quick! She sold off her furniture in a yard sale to buy her some breathing room while she figured out what to do next.

Her neighbor, who had helped her move her sofa to the front lawn, admired her gutsiness and determination so much that he offered to make room for her in his real estate firm.

She leveraged her experience there to become a general manager of a business and vacation resort in Florida. Not only did she excel at taking care of details for the guests, but she really enjoyed it, bringing an unbridled passion and innovative approach to her work that won her many accolades from her employers and customers alike. Confident that she had great concepts to sell, she decided to put a price tag on her ideas, just like she had on that sofa in the yard sale years earlier.

She pitched her ideas to the decision-makers at the Ritz-Carlton, Omni, and Plaza hotels, all known for their attention to detail. They bought into her plan, allowing Linda's team of independent inspectors to look into every function of the hotel's business to make sure that each was being performed to the highest standards in providing guest services. How long does a bar patron have to wait before being served? Is the room service speedy and reliable? Are guests informed about the hotel services? Are receptionists polite? How long does it take to check in and check out? Like my own business, Linda Novey Enterprises was born from adversity but cultivated by creativity.

Neither Linda nor I created a better mousetrap, or any kind of tangible goods for that matter (though I sell cars, building them is not part of my creative business plan). A common misconception about creativity is that it's limited to the actual creation of a product. But once the "creative team" produces the product, it's the marketing, image-making, customer relations, and business systems that can make or break a business. For most entrepreneurs, applying creativity to these vital activities is essential—paying attention to details, using your active intuition, thinking outside the box—all these are, in fact, elements that come together to define creativity.

The account of Linda Novey's experience and the other stories that appear in these pages aren't designed to provide a course in creativity but are meant to inspire you to be fearless in your own pursuits. (If I slip in a few gems from my collection of 101 Creative Ideas for the Workplace, I do so with the intent of stimulating your creative juices.)

Creativity flows from active intuition. When you take what you've observed and act upon it, you can take control of your own world and claim a stake in the world at large.

Creativity as a Function of Change

Have you ever watched youngsters entertain themselves with only a few props and their unlimited imaginations? They aren't bound by any rules and they aren't afraid to remake their world to their own liking. Unfettered by expectations or the risk of embarrassment, children have the most actively creative lives imaginable. But the world has a way of stifling creativity and forcing us into paths of conformity as we grow older. We tend to take the road most traveled because that's where we feel safe. To break out of a predictable cycle of behavior can be scary. It takes courage to say, "I'm going to try something new."

Like the infant who fearlessly explores a new world—and eventually takes command of it with her first steps—creativity brings about change. When we look beyond the confines of our problems, solutions only become evident when we free ourselves to think differently and push into the realm of the unknown.

Maria de Lourdes Sobrino, whose nickname is Lulu, grew up in Mexico City, got her college degree in business administration, and, following her childhood dream to move to the United States, relocated to Los Angeles to open a branch of her Mexico City–based travel and convention management company. Then a deep recession in Mexico hit the business hard, and it failed.

Determined to stay in the United States, she came up with a new, and unrelated, business idea. Her own mother's kitchen was the place she found inspiration with the humble gelatin desserts that she remembered so fondly from her childhood. She also recognized the growing interest in ethnic foods in the United States and, presto, she created Lulu's Desserts. In the beginning she prepared 300 cups each night in her own kitchen and distributed them to local shops on consignment each morning. Within three years, Lulu's Desserts became a multimillion-dollar enterprise. Maria now operates out of a 70,000-square-foot plant. She is now working on her next phase, which is to take the company public.

Although Maria's creativity came into full bloom when circumstances conspired to destroy her lifelong dream, she was not simply reacting to her situation; she turned a crisis into an opportunity using her intuition and creativity.

To me, expressing creativity is a deliberate revolutionary

act, committed to upset an existing order. Pioneers in every field of endeavor have been creative, whether they're exploring the wilds of cyberspace, pushing the boundaries in the arts, or simply trying to find a means to survive. Maria let her vision guide her in the face of some overwhelming obstacles; she bounced back from a failed business, she nurtured herself and her dream, she activated her intuition to discover and develop a unique business, and she used every creative bone to make it happen.

Making Creativity Work for You

Those who have a thing to sell

and go and whisper in a well

aren't so apt to get the dollars

as one who climbs a tree and hollers.

—FORTUNE COOKIE WISDOM

No matter how good your ideas may be, a low-profile, play-it-safe approach to any endeavor will keep you on the sidelines. One of my greatest frustrations is hearing women say, "I've got some super ideas for a business, but . . ." But what? It makes me want to kick their butts. So many women will set up obstacles to their own success—and one of the biggest is their fear of self-promotion.

Self-promotion is not simply bragging. It's largely about

image making. And who better than a woman to understand image. Most of us look in the mirror every day and create an image—what's all that stuff in your makeup bag for anyway? And what about those matching shoes and belts and scarves? It's all about image. The packaging of products and services influences today's consumers almost as much as the function or quality. Goods as diverse as perfume and cars are marketed as much on promises—of beauty, wealth, prestige, or pleasure—as they are on their inherent value.

That's why fashioning a credible and distinctive image and promoting yourself and your company is such powerful stuff. I venture to say if you come up with a stand-out-from-the-pack company concept, you're well on your way to becoming a successful entrepreneur.

Remember when you were a little girl, how cute it was to be a showoff. I'm reminded of my niece, who, when she was about four or five years old, used to prepare a special dance routine for family get-togethers Randi would stand in the middle of the den and wiggle and skip and hop about like a budding Dallas Cowboy cheerleader. We'd all clap and clamor for more.

Then, as she got older, six or seven, she'd recite poems that she wrote for every occasion. They were truly precious. Now, as she "matures," seldom do we get a peek at Little Miss Showoff. Last Christmas we asked her to recite one of her poems and she looked at us like we were all from another planet. What happened?

Somewhere in the process of a girl's becoming a woman, what is considered to be acceptable behavior changes. Whether it's peer pressure or society's expectations, women are still drawn to the supporting roles in life—mother and helpmate—where her nurturing nature feels most comfortable. Yet so often these roles are devalued and the very qualities that women bring to them are underappreciated in the business world.

At first, self-promotion may make you feel uncomfortable but getting noticed doesn't mean that you have to dance around the room like my niece (there are other ways to embrace your creative inner child). You don't have to transform yourself into a circus act to draw attention to what you are doing. A case in point is Nicole Wild's journey from successful fund-raiser to entrepreneur who never lost touch with her deep sense of social responsibility.

Nicole, an attractive thirty-something, moved to the United States from Australia in 1996. As a champion fund-raiser, she imported not only her organizational experience but also her compassion for other less fortunate women. Once settled in her adopted country, she signed on as a volunteer for Suited for Success, a nonprofit organization that helps women on welfare get back to work. She was soon promoted to a paid position and during her two-year stint as a fund-raising director she organized imaginative benefits, including a celebrity suit donation (boasting contributions from television talk show hosts Rosie O'Donnell and Oprah Winfrey). Her take-notice event was a front-page success.

As an intuitive and creative extension of her work with Suited for Success, she recently launched Nikaya Inc., an aromatherapy soap business, with the express purpose of helping women get off the welfare roles and find meaningful employment. Nicole's products, once made in her kitchen, are now distributed nationally in luxury spas and hotel gift shops.

In 1999, *Cosmopolitan* magazine applauded Nicole's altruistic endeavors by naming her its Fun, Fearless Female of the Year.

God Is in the Details

Be concerned about every aspect of the way that your business is packaged, from its name to its location to how you present yourself to colleagues and customers alike. God is, as they say, in the details and there is no greater opportunity to express your creativity than through these small things.

Each of my image-making and marketing plans started with the naming of my business. When I opened my first car dealership, I knew I wanted the sign above the door to have more appeal than just my own name. I conjured up—and then discarded—Friendly Motors and Courtesy Chrysler among many others. Why settle for friendly or courteous, I decided, when you can be loving? And so Love Chrysler was christened. *Love*, to me, is the most positive word in our vocabulary. When I set out to create a company name and logo, I knew that it was an opportunity to reveal my philosophy about business and about my life. (Can you imagine any man calling his business Love?)

I designed my company's logo to be an eye-catcher—"Love" engraved on a heart. In a sense, an automobile dealer's logo is a minibillboard placed on the back of every car we sell. I've had customers actually tell me that our logo brought them in the door. I took the idea a step further by advertising that it's not just our cars that have big hearts; so do our people.

But I was reminded recently by my receptionist of a time when my own creativity misfired, hitting something other than the target I was aiming for. When I first started Love Chrysler, I requested the phone number 994-LOVE. I wanted a phone number that jumped off the page and would leave an imprint in people's minds. I then eagerly launched an advertising campaign appealing to potential customers to "Dial 99 for LOVE." Only one hitch. I kept losing receptionists. I couldn't figure out why until one brave girl—on her way out the door—told me she was leaving because of our "ridiculous phone number." It seems that floods of obscene phone calls had been pouring in. This was obviously not the kind of image I was trying to create. I was forced to change it. The new number, 991-LOVE, is not as memorable but at least I'm not going through receptionists like before.

Creating ways to surprise and please your customers provides other opportunities to stand out from the pack. I know a real estate associate who uses a simple tool to do just that. This enterprising saleswoman fills a small ice chest each morning on hot summer days with a wide variety of cold beverages. The well-stocked ice chest provides quite a treat for her clients as they climb in and out of the hot car while house hunting.

Designing—and using—just the right business card is an often overlooked but important detail in business. One salesman I know had the back of his cards imprinted with "100 gallons of gasoline FREE with auto purchase" (remember that men can be innovative, too). One customer later told him that she bought a car from him because his card was the only one she had kept. It's true. If you offer someone a just-in-case reason to keep your card, they probably will.

And if you're a one-woman show, you'll want to consider a technique that many "virtual" companies use and take some inspiration from a former marketing vice president for an Internet service provider. She had been contemplating going out on her own for some time but getting demoted (even though that's not what her boss called it) thrust her into action. It was a blessing in disguise anyway because she had been suffering from anxiety and worry over the merger trend in the industry. She decided that she needed to take control of her own destiny.

Her first challenge in launching her computer consulting service was to create a perception of a not-so-small business. She tackled each facet of her start-up so that every detail had impact.

The basics weren't optional: a fax machine, an E-mail address and (especially given the nature of her business) a website. Her business stationery was elegant and professionally printed. She subscribed to an answering service that didn't sound like an answering service (she *never* answered her own phone). She arranged to have a time-share conference room in a downtown bank building for important meetings. And she set up her business to accept credit cards because she knew that initially she'd be taking on some smaller clients with cash-flow issues like her own.

With her background in marketing, she promoted her services aggressively yet efficiently, cashing in some of her personal IOUs with the media from her previous position. By the end of her second month, she was up and running and even profitable. No one has a clue that she operates out of a spare bedroom—oftentimes dressed in her bathrobe. (I promised I wouldn't tell that last bit, so I'm not giving her name here.)

I'm a believer. The woman's touch—creative attention to details—has been a huge plus in my business. I've learned that sweating the small stuff can make a big difference in business—not to mention that it garners the kind of applause my niece enjoyed when she danced around the den!

All of the women who've shared their experiences in this book have drawn on their innate strengths—those beautiful truths about women—including their creative resources. Each chose to leave the cocoon of convention and let her creativity thrive. Active intuition alerted them all to the challenges ahead, and then they set out to create solutions to those problems.

An entrepreneur's primary business is to provide alternatives. Active intuition and creativity allow you to identify and implement those alternatives. But for most women entrepreneurs, providing a service, a product, or an alternative becomes much more than a job. The venture into the world of self-employment may have been prompted by necessity, but it is fueled by passion.

seven

Passion

Passion is our deepest, strongest emotion. It is the energy that drives and sustains our enthusiasm not only to pursue those activities for which we have a natural aptitude or in which we are intensely interested, but for life itself.

In the male-dominated business world, the importance of emotions has generally been ignored, at best, and scorned, at worst. However, virtually all the successful women I know have told me they "made it" because passion was a driving force within them. Time and again, women show that their passion is the root from which their successes grow.

Defining Passion

Psychologists say there is an important connection between our emotions and our beliefs. If you feel anger, it comes from an underlying belief that in some way you have been treated unfairly. What beliefs create the feeling of passion? Passion is sparked by the belief that something is worthwhile or needs doing. Passion is supported by your confidence in abilities that you can do what needs to be done. And finally, passion animates your belief in a dream or vision of what can be achieved.

Passion does not need great displays of emotion to thrive. It can live quietly within the person who, without fanfare or self-aggrandizement, can stay focused on a problem until a solution is found. Passion is not limited to operatic performance but can be found in the humblest domestic drama.

Redefining Failure

Growing up, Elizabeth Hopkins spent many hours teaching her autistic sister, Dana, how to sing and play the piano. Elizabeth's fervent conviction about the importance of art and music in the lives of the disabled led her to apply for a position to teach music at a special education school in Virginia.

When she first applied for the job, she was bluntly informed that the school only hired teachers with master's degrees. Although she was an accomplished musician, Elizabeth hadn't even finished her undergraduate degree.

After a few months, she heard that the newly hired teacher had left the school without notice, literally running, screaming out the door. Elizabeth reapplied but was again told that they "preferred" someone with a master's degree. The second music teacher lasted only six months. Elizabeth applied a third time. This time she got the job, but only as a "substitute."

On her first day, Elizabeth faced a roomful of broken instruments and a class of students whose disabilities ranged from autism to attention deficit disorder. She soon realized that the previous teachers had tried to apply a single system to a wide variety of students with disastrous results. In spite of Elizabeth's lack of academic qualifications and experience, the school administrators avoided visiting the classroom for several months. They just seemed to be relieved that at the beginning of each day she was still at her post. When they finally got around to looking in on one of her classes, they couldn't help but express their astonishment. Elizabeth had managed to develop the first successful music program in the school's history.

Elizabeth's "temporary" position lasted three years, during which time she also created both a library and a theater in her class, writing and directing several plays a year with the children. When she left, she asked the administrators if her replacement would be required to have a master's degree. They answered, "No, we want to hire someone just like you."

Passion is the catalyst that helps us recognize our dreams. It acts as a driving force that energizes and supports us to create and nurture what we believe in. Because of a childhood relationship, Elizabeth developed a belief that something was worth doing. She had confidence that she could do it and she had a dream of what she could achieve. Passion changes the definition of failure from "not succeeding" to "not trying."

Overcoming Obstacles

Passion doesn't remove obstacles but it does ignite our courage to overcome them or at least maneuver around them. It takes courage to look past the roadblocks as well as break down self-imposed boundaries.

Dr. Virginia Apgar is one such pioneer. As a medical student in the 1940s, she was discouraged from pursuing her dream to become a surgeon because at the time it was considered not to be a field appropriate for women. But she forged ahead in obstetrics, where her passion to heal and her nurturing temperament came together to change the course of neonatal care forever. Her deep concern for the babies who were carried off to nurseries immediately after birth with no evaluation of their health led her to develop a simple procedure that today still carries her name, the Apgar score. Her test makes it possible to identify quickly at-risk babies and ensure prompt medical attention. Universal use of the Apgar score has been responsible for reducing unnecessary suffering in thousands of infants and dramatically lowering mortality rates.

Virginia Apgar embodied the "entrepreneurial" spirit and in the face of some pretty stiff opposition, pursued her passion with remarkable results. For the rest of us, embracing our passion is the first step toward fulfilling our hearts' desires.

Finding Your Passion

I've heard some women say that they don't "know enough" to unleash their passion. I am not suggesting that pure passion is all you'll need to launch a business, but passion is the best catalyst I know for action. To start this nuclear reaction, you don't need all of the answers. And the fact is you'll never have all the answers. Your plan doesn't need to be perfect or even complete. If that were true, I'd still be back in my personal Stone Age.

Before you can give your all to something, you've got to know what's in your heart. Sometimes what's there is only revealed when you are at your lowest point or when the world seems to be falling down around you. Through the pain and confusion, when everything else is stripped away, you finally recognize that you've got nothing left but belief in yourself.

Beginning with my diagnosis of cervical cancer, it seemed that I was hit with one calamity after another. I could have very easily become a victim, staying in the passenger's seat and leaving my fate in the hands of others. I could have just hoped for the best and gone on wishing that my fortunes were other than what they were. But my passion for life and for giving to other people was still very much alive, and that passion fueled my courage to take charge of my life.

I'm no Saint Marion, but I do believe that the purpose of life is to contribute to and share in the lives of others. For me, that realization made me understand and eventually channel the energy of my passion, first into motherhood and then into my business.

When I was at the crossroad of can and cannot, I knew that I needed to determine what was in my heart with the greatest clarity. I had to examine my life to find those events that had given me a sense of pride and joy. I wrote them down. Then I looked for a common theme.

Setting aside the two days I gave birth to my two sons— events that are in a league of their own—I recalled six or seven experiences when I felt truly alive. Reclaiming these experiences helped me to feel an inner peace as I became reacquainted with who I really was. I started to see myself again as a leader with a nurturing soul and an organizer with a creative spirit. The realization that I had enormous gifts to share with others illuminated the darkness of my lack of purpose and feeling of hopelessness.

When you revisit past experiences in your life and recollect the times when you felt most passionate about or connected to something, you will inevitably discover the qualities common to them. How can you infuse those same qualities into your work life today? And why is it so important? For many women in business, and particularly for the woman entrepreneur, making a living is more than just earning a wage. It is about having more choices and control over your life, about feeling pride in your accomplishments, and about having the freedom to express and give shape to your dreams.

Living Your Passion

When I first went into the workforce I wasn't thinking about my passion beyond feeding two small boys and keeping a roof over our heads. As it turned out, that instinct for survival and to protect my family would be a guiding force throughout my life. I daresay it's the same for most women. But once the crisis was over and I was able to indulge in a few moments of self-reflection, I accepted that my mission in life, my passion for life, was wrapped up in what I could do for other people. Just as we women may be prone to put too much stock in what others think about us (but more on that later) I recognized that I invested a lot in thinking about others. If my goal in life is to make a difference, then I can't do that without doing for others. It's a characteristic that I share with most women.

A few years ago, I picked up a newspaper and began reading an article about gang violence in our community. My teenage son walked in and asked why I was so "down." By way of response, I read him the nauseating story about gangs of teenagers vandalizing homes.

That started a conversation about how so many good teenagers got a "bad rap" for the actions of a few. He told me how just that very day, he had noticed that an elderly woman held her purse more closely when he entered an elevator with her. I felt outraged that this pattern of media reporting—"bad stuff"—was giving people a distorted perception of the youth in our community.

I had a choice. I could sit and stew about it or I could try to make something positive come out of my belief that the media was creating an unrealistic picture of teenagers. The instinct to protect the reputations of my teenage sons—and by extension the thousands of other good kids out there—was nearly as strong as the one to feed and protect them as little ones. But what could I do to solve this problem? I believed that this was a worthwhile cause and I believed that I should and could do something about it.

My son and I began to shoot ideas back and forth. We ended up initiating a program to recognize civic-minded high school students in Texas. Here's how it worked: Each week one boy and one girl were selected and featured in a Texas newspaper as the "Love Chrysler Top High School Student of the Week." At the end of the school year, a student was selected from the pool of weekly honorees, and that deserving student was named the "Love Chrysler Top High School Student of the Year" and became the recipient of a brand-new car.

News of the program made headlines. Several radio stations promoted it. When the first car was awarded, the television stations ran it as their lead-in piece. And the public got to read stories about teenagers volunteering at nursing homes that preempted the stories about young hoodlums vandalizing homes.

Creating this initiative was as important to me as any corporate plan, sales incentive, or advertising campaign that I could have dreamed up to promote my business. It brought together every aspect of my life—my desire to protect my sons, my intense interest in righting wrongs, and my zeal to run a business with a conscience. It's impossible for me to separate my personal beliefs from my business interests and it would be a betrayal for me to do otherwise. Being in charge of my own affairs allows me to do what I feel is right and it's what gives a voice to my passions.

Sharing Your Passion

It's one thing to recognize and act upon your passions, but it takes more than a little enthusiastic cheerleading to bring others on board—to share your passion and to encourage them to share their cash so your business can get going.

It was less than five years since I'd sold my first car when I started feeling an itch to go out on my own. I wanted to create a woman's brand of car dealership. My passion to do so fueled my courage to conjure up a daring plan to make my dream come true.

I decided to ask an executive from Chrysler Corporation how much money I would need to start up my own agency. We met for lunch at his private club. After a little chitchat, I popped the question.

"Eight hundred thousand dollars," he replied bluntly.

He may as well have said $800 billion. If I sold my belongings and my soul, I might have been able to come up with a few thousand—not even enough to buy a car, let alone a car dealership. I took a bite of salmon so that I'd have something to do with my mouth other than to let it hang open.

Yet I left that lunch undaunted, with my plan to be my own boss intact. I had no money but I had a belief in myself. I just needed someone to share it with me. Someone with money.

Over the years, I had received a lot of praise for my work—certificates of achievement, commendations, and press clippings. These accolades had impressed my customers so I figured that maybe they would impress a potential investor, so I created a portfolio, a kind of brag folder, with a cover letter, which basically said, "Here's your chance." I mailed out about twenty packages to CPAs and financial planners in my area.

Two weeks later I received a phone call from my future

partner. We met and struck a deal on the spot. He described me as "unstoppable." My quest for capital was rewarded in part because I showed off the results of a little sweat equity, but mostly because I made my passion contagious. (I also paid him off with interest within two years!)

The start-up capital I raised did not buy an existing car dealership. It simply served as evidence to Chrysler Corporation that I was monetarily qualified to receive a franchise. All I had was a piece of paper, a large debt, and a dream. The next step was to build a team that would not only share that dream, and my passion, but would make it a reality.

Creating the Dream Team

When I was putting together my "dream team," I assumed that everyone I hired would share the passion that I had. Why else would they come to work with me? I certainly didn't hold back sharing my vision with my prospective employees, both men and women, for a different kind of car dealership. But that assumption was one of the first mistakes I made in business.

Early indicators showed that my organization was not running efficiently. It appeared that my employees lacked motivation. Didn't they get it? This was supposed to be a business where love filled the air like music, where time clocks weren't necessary and bad moods gave way to smiles. I soon realized that they weren't sharing my vision.

I knew there must be something I could do to infuse some life into my people. I wrestled with the problem, desperately looking for some model on which I could shape my organization. Curiously, I became intrigued with—are you ready for this?—General George Patton! The most macho of the macho was about to become the poster boy for my woman-centered business.

Patton was a master at making his men feel that his dream was their dream. He understood that a person rarely develops the confidence to strive for greatness if their small achievements go unacknowledged. His simple rule for using the pronoun *you*—as in "*You* have captured 140,112 enemy soldiers" or "*You* have taken the high ground"—went a long way to giving his men the incentive for accomplishment.

Like Patton, I had to recognize and use the unique talents of my employees and let their vision have a place within mine.

I learned the value of praise to lift the human spirit and the rewards that could come by making someone feel that their dream was part of a greater dream. What a turnaround! Positive feedback had made all the difference. We soon began to live up to our name, Love Chrysler.

Selling Your Passion

I strongly believe that entrepreneurial businesses offer incredible opportunities for women because it gives them the best chance to sell their passion. Because of women's capacity for empathy, our unique ability to really listen, to tune in to and share the passions of others, we can thrive in this world driven by selling.

The great thing about selling is that you can fulfill the dreams and desires of others while achieving your own! Whether your goals involve gaining financial security, having an independent career, or finding a strong sense of personal accomplishment, working in sales can help you on your way.

A while back, I met a man who owns a company that markets private aircraft. "Even though most of my customers are men," he confided, "women are my best salesmen. They're better than men are because they know how to speak to what people really want. The men on my sales force spend too much time on the technical, mechanical stuff with the customers. A woman, on the other hand, establishes a rapport with the customer."

He went on to explain that everyone on the sales staff understood that if the customer is a technophile, they should certainly be able to speak to that. But instinctively the women understood that a private airplane often meant much more than a means to get from one place to another quickly. That aircraft could fulfill a man's desire for freedom and independence. What if he wants to take off impulsively to the Bahamas so he can indulge his passion for snorkeling? What if he just wants to impress his in-laws? A woman, with her "empathy gene," can discern the customer's needs and quickly tailor her sales approach.

Since a woman's intuition helps her to "read" customers, to know what moves them, she is better able to communicate with them. We are rarely in a position to sit a customer down and run them through a complete personality profile test, but we still need to know the answers to questions beyond the obvious—questions that address the customers' desires—in order to tap into customers' needs.

What excites your customers, what taps into their passions, should always take precedence over what excites you. I am reminded of the time when one of my salesmen was going on and on with a female customer about the new engine featured in the current model year of the car she was looking at. After she left (without buying), he ridiculed her because she seemed more interested in the beverage holders than she did in the engine. He missed the point—and more important, the sale. In his presentation, he had breezed right past the beverage holders, which had more value in her eyes than the engine!

Whether we are selling an airplane, a car, or a trip to the moon, getting to know our customer shows us how our product or service fits into a customer's lifestyle, fulfills his or her hopes and dreams and even fantasies. Without getting to know the customer, we can't really know what we're selling because we don't really fully comprehend what the customer is "buying."

As entrepreneurs and as salespeople, it should be our passion to connect with the needs of our customers. The real bonus in making the sale is not just a commission, but a sense of having made the connection, of having earned prosperity by truly speaking to the customer's needs. When we believe in our product and tune in to the customer's needs and desires, we will inevitably find that we have enriched their lives and, it follows, our own.

Giving Voice to Your Passion

Our lives have purpose when we are able to respond not only to our personal wants and needs, but to those of the world as well. Entrepreneurial urges speak to us from our hearts, telling us we have something to offer. "I am meant to do something with my life" is the cry from the voice inside.

Passion is a generator. It drives us past the stagnancy of wishin' and hopin', through the planning phases, and around the obstacles and challenges, and across the peaks and valleys, until plans and hopes become reality.

Putting passion into your work turns a simple moneymaking project into something that brings purpose and power into your life. Acknowledging passion transforms your hopes and wishes into reality. Unleashing passion sets you on the road to explore new horizons, overcome difficulties, and find solutions to problems you never thought possible. Embracing your passion makes you reconsider how you direct your work and your life.

Nothing in your life has to remain the same if that's not the way you want it to be. Through your passion you will find the courage to take risks and to create the life you're worthy of living.

Part 3

eight

Self-Value

Living an authentic life where our passion guides us toward purpose is the highest measure any of us can enjoy. But often it is not the standard we use to gauge our own worth. Instead, we tend to care so much about how other people see us that we lose sight of our real self and therefore our real worth.

Both men and women wrestle with the issue of self-worth. That's because both genders use a means of self-identity to measure their own value. But traditionally they have differed in how they have done this. Men primarily identify themselves according to what they do for a living and women see themselves, first and foremost, in terms of their relationships.

In interactions with hundreds of customers, I noticed that men and women relate to themselves differently. I did not set out to conduct a gender study, but the results were pretty clear.

Every other month, my auto agency hosts a casual get-acquainted evening for new customers. These "Right from the Start" events provide an opportunity for the new vehicle owners to meet members of our service team. In the course of the function, we survey customers to learn more about their individual transportation needs. One of the questions we ask is "Are you the primary driver of the new car? If yes, identify the most important role in your life that your new car will serve."

Here are a few responses from the men:

"I am an environmental consultant and will be dependent on this vehicle for my field calls."

"As an architect, I frequently travel to job sites."

"As a pharmaceutical sales representative, I will be putting many highway miles on this vehicle."

Responses from women:

"I will be taking three eleven-year-olds to and from school as I am in a car pool. I am also a real estate agent."

"I take care of my disabled mother, running errands such as grocery shopping for her, as well as commuting fifty miles roundtrip five days per week to my full-time job."

"I am the team mother for our school's cheerleading squad and an English teacher."

The pattern of these responses emerged as a definition of the major ways in which the sexes self-identify: men, primarily through their work, and women, fundamentally through their relationships. The survey may as well be asking, "What is your primary role in life?" or "How do you see yourself?"

This is not to say that men don't think of themselves as fathers, husbands, sons, or brothers. They just don't seem to use those roles as their predominant means of self-identity. And my assessment doesn't imply that women don't cherish their careers; it just concludes that women, in general, think in terms of being mothers, daughters, wives, or whatever first, relating to their careers in an almost oh-by-the-way kind of fashion.

The link between self-identification and self-worth might explain why many men lean toward being workaholics and so many women are compulsive helpers. For both sexes, the road to self-esteem is often paved with other people's opinions.

For women, measuring our worth based on our personal relationships is not inherently wrong. What is noteworthy, however, is how it affects us in the business world where low value has traditionally been placed on "women's work"— whether it's in the home or at support jobs in the workplace. Maybe you've heard that the "R" jobs—HR and PR—are often considered to be dead ends, rarely leading to positions of executive authority. Human resources and public relations jobs are typically not highly valued positions—in terms of money anyway—in the corporate world. Relationship or people skills, unless they're applied in sales, are often underrated.

And because women tend not to make their careers the center of their universe, it makes it tough to compete in business with men who do. However, the landscape is changing as the line between work and the rest of our life becomes blurred—and nowhere is this more evident than for entrepreneurs.

In a service-oriented market, a woman's love (and need) for relationships can be very valuable. Being considerate of what others think is healthy and certainly very useful in building effective communication. But a self-identity based solely on relationships—one where happiness and destiny is placed in the hands of others—can lead to a low self-worth.

When the approval of others dictates your every move and when you need accolades and prizes to validate your existence, you'll find yourself yo-yoing from high to low, and the sure result is an injured self-esteem.

And when you're reliant on personal relationships as a sole measure of your own worth, you're bound to have difficulty accepting simple praise. It follows that you would feel unworthy of it when you're maneuvering through life with low-valued traits. For me, one of the qualities I admire most in myself is my maternal nurturing style. But there was a time when I felt that I had to apologize for it. It was only when I accepted my nurturing side as a strength that I realized a confident woman claims her right to receive praise—and even sing her own. I also realized that confident, nurturing women build strong companies.

Another relationship-based self-identity hazard is linked to our tendency for constant comparison of ourselves to others. It places us at risk of losing our ability to embrace our authenticity. Your true self is bound to be in hiding if you're living a life designed to keep up with and impress other people.

What we think of ourselves affects every aspect of our personal and professional lives. For the woman who lacks a belief in her right to be happy, the world can be a very dreary place. For the woman who lacks a belief in her ability to cope with life's challenges, the world can be a very scary place. By contrast, a woman who fundamentally believes in herself is one who's likely to realize her full potential.

Needing the Approval of Others

When I was a teenager, if I asked to stay home on a school day or have a boyfriend over past ten P.M., my mother's typical comment would be, "What will the neighbors think?" I still have this vision of our "neighbors" glued to their windows with their binoculars watching my every move. My mother, of course, wanted to measure up as a good mother in their eyes. Her need for the neighbors' approval often dictated her life and, by extension, mine.

Caring about what other people think of you is normal. It can even be a good thing. That is, when you don't allow it to burn positive energy. Craving the approval of others can be so debilitating that it takes over your thought processes.

I recall a day when I allowed my need for approval to overwhelm my sense of pragmatic thinking. Driving to work for what was to be my first day on the job to sell cars, was I dreaming up creative ways I might be able to announce my new position to friends and acquaintances? No. Was I formulating a plan to persuade the mortgage company to grant me an extension? No. Was I thinking about how I would be getting my sons to and from school in the immediate future? Nope. I had only one concern: What if they don't like me? The "they," of course, that I was obsessing about was the group of men I would be calling my peers. I wanted their approval so much that all of my legitimate concerns were—temporarily, only, thank goodness—suspended.

What I've since come to realize is that when you live your life guided by the opinions of other people, you're actually relinquishing your own personal power. Women are natural pleasers so this is a tough concept for us to grasp. But think about it: If your boss or business partner knows that your primary goal is to be liked, how does that knowledge have an impact when you're negotiating a raise or a partnership agreement? If your employees know you've got to be liked, you'll soon be the owner of a company where the tail's wagging the dog.

The surest way for you to be held hostage in any situation is to allow yourself to be governed by the insatiable need for approval. The surest way to deplete your positive mental energy is to allow yourself to be consumed with "I hope they like me" thinking. And the surest way to lose your own sense of worth is to attach it to the opinions of others.

If you're grounded in who you really are, *apart* from your relationships, you'll find you're better able to nurture all relationships. A healthy self-esteem is like a shock absorber for life, making you more resilient and able to bounce back from the bumps along life's path. If you're not distracted by trying to fulfill someone else's idea of what you're supposed to be, you'll find yourself being more attentive to all that life has to offer. Your intuition will be on full alert. You'll be free to create your own identity fueled by your own passion.

Feeling Unworthy of Praise

"That's a lovely suit," a woman is told.

"Do you like it?" she replies.

Have you ever noticed that so many women have a hard time accepting a compliment? We want to hear it repeated and restated as though we're in disbelief. We feel undeserving. Men typically accept praise with a sense of entitlement. They behave as though they just scored a point; women act as if they've committed a fraud.

And even worse, I've observed women who take a compliment and use it as a frame in which to insert an unflattering picture of themselves. Just today, I overheard a man compliment his secretary on her preparation of a great report. She answered by telling him that she should have made it more detailed. She added that she didn't feel "all that good" about it. Obviously, what she didn't feel all that good about was herself. When we don't feel good about ourselves on the inside, it doesn't much matter what we achieve or accomplish; we're not going to feel a sense of confidence or worthiness. Even my very first sale, which proved to be a remarkable feat under the circumstances, left me feeling unworthy of praise. On that day, I strode purposefully into the showroom to greet a giant, surly looking, pot-bellied, big-bearded man sporting suspenders. Here in Texas we call them Bubbas. The first thing he said to me was, "Lady, I've been buyin' new cars for thirty years. I've never bought one car from a woman and I'm not about to start today."

"Gee, you've got me beat," I said. "You've been buying them for thirty years and I've only been selling them for thirty minutes." Later that day he drove away the owner of a brand-new car—the first one he ever bought from a woman.

When my peers later praised me for making a "tough sale," I scoffed at them by saying that I had lucked out. I convinced myself (and them) that the man had chosen to do business with me because he thought he could take advantage of the situation. In hindsight, maybe he was so taken aback by my candor that he knew I wouldn't be taking advantage of him.

Frankly, that first sale didn't do much to bolster my confidence for future endeavors since I believed that I had faked my way to success. But experience has taught me that I am worthy of praise when it comes my way and I have learned to accept it, as Forrest Gump would say, as one of life's little "chawklits." That is to say, it's a good thing, but I don't need it to survive.

Comparing One's Self to Others

When I attended the Avon Women of Enterprise Awards Ceremony in New York City, I heard Whoopi Goldberg say, "I love [recognition] programs that give women the knowledge that other women are creating new things. You know how women are. If one is doing it, you can bet another one is going to want to try!"

Because we base our self-worth on our self-identity and

because our self-identity is based on our relationships, comparing ourselves to others is natural. Comparisons can motivate us to stretch and learn. Used right, they can be a positive force in our lives.

When I was in the first grade, I was in the "Stars," the first of three reading groups in my class. My best friend was placed in the middle group. She would tell me how every night she practiced reading because she wanted to be in the "Stars" too. She eventually made it. It's very possible that her entire educational experience was enhanced because she made good use of the comparison.

Looking at women (and men) who are accomplishing feats that you feel you too can manage can be a source of inspiration. That's healthy.

But it can be otherwise when comparisons result in feelings of discouragement and even resentment. "I get depressed when I see women on TV much younger than I am who have accomplished so much," says a forty-something receptionist at a bank. When feelings of deprivation crowd out feelings of contentment, comparisons are not being used constructively. If learning of someone else's success makes you feel like a failure, you're engaged in destructive thinking.

And when you're comparing what you have with what another woman has, be honest with yourself. Do you wish you were at a place where another woman is in life—with all it took her to get there and all it takes for her to stay there?

Women looking in from the outside envy Faith, a very

successful buyer for a high-end retail department store. She seems to have it all. She has a beautiful apartment overlooking Central Park in New York City. She frequently travels around the world. She loves her career. The hitch? Her husband, a partner in a prominent law firm, loves his job too. His practice is in Los Angeles!

Comparison making is a fact of life. There's nothing wrong with admiring other people and even trying to emulate them. After all, camping out only in relationships that make you feel superior can stifle your personal and professional growth. But be on the lookout for the comparison trap. It comes alive when we look at what others are doing and then allow ourselves to adopt a sense of shame or self-pity because we don't think we're measuring up. There's nothing to be gained by making these kinds of comparisons and everything to lose—namely our self-esteem.

Relying on the approval of other people is a by-product of seeing ourselves through their eyes. And when we don't believe in the value of our inherent abilities, talents, and contributions, we feel unworthy of praise. We also find ourselves in a state of making constant comparisons, which causes us to lose sight of who we're really meant to be. These behaviors are the dark side of relationship-based self-identification because they can provoke a feeling of low self-worth. But there are ways to develop strengths for building or rebuilding a healthy self-esteem.

Be True to Yourself

No matter what business you're in, getting other people on board requires that they have a belief in you. And selling your vision can only be achieved by being true to yourself. Impostors are quickly uncovered. The smell of insincerity is so strong that it can't be masked by the scent of even the most charming act.

The number one reason women (and men) "put on airs," as they say in the South, is that they lack self-confidence. When you feel that your knowledge, intelligence, and ability to accomplish something are less than adequate, you'll be tempted to borrow what you've seen work for someone else.

A few years ago, I received an invitation to attend a retirement party for a corporate big cheese—to be hosted on a cruise liner off the coast of Monte Carlo, no less. Immediately, I called a couple of girlfriends to share my excitement. Their first question was, "What are you going to wear?" All of a sudden, it became a huge concern to me too. Of course as you might guess, nothing in my closet was good enough. Rather than rely on my own judgment to shop for an outfit, I let my friends dress me. One of them had just the perfect pantsuit—never mind that I would have felt more "me" in a dress. Another friend had the perfect jewelry—never mind that it was totally "not me."

Decked out in a borrowed ensemble, I climbed aboard

the yacht. What I discovered was that the disingenuous way I had dressed myself really undermined my self-confidence. The evening, while not a disaster, was a strain, namely because I felt like a phony.

If you're putting up a false front, it's evident you distrust the "real you" to do the job. It could also mean that you lack trust in the person or people that you're trying to fool. Maybe they've expressed disapproval or intolerance of the "real you" in the past. But when you go into hiding—and that's what a façade is—you're subliminal message to yourself is that you're not a worthwhile person or that there's something wrong with you. Come out of hiding and say, "Take me for who I am." Why on earth would you want to associate with people who like you for what you're not anyway?

After all, to be your best, you need to give yourself the freedom to be you. And using someone else's life as a strict model for what yours should be suppresses your sense of individualism. A woman who personifies the motto "To thine own self be true" is Katharine Hepburn.

She's a woman who traded in Hollywood glamour for a comfortable pair of slacks she personally preferred—at a time when women didn't wear pants. Throughout her life, she honored her spirit of individualism. And even though—or more than likely because—she was her own woman, it's apparent that her contemporaries more than approved of her; they admired her. They bestowed twelve Oscar nominations on her and a nickname that says it all: "Kate the Great."

I'm personally acquainted with another great lady who is able to look in the mirror and see an authentic reflection. That's because she found success using her own dream as a model. Deborah Rosado Shaw, who grew up in the South Bronx, the nation's poorest congressional district, didn't pattern her life after anyone else's. She accepted encouraging words from supporters along the way, but her role model was her belief in—and vision of—her own potential.

She recalls how her early ambitions were to eat brand-name foods, stay warm, and feel safe from gang members. But her grandmother—who washed floors at the Waldorf-Astoria Hotel in New York City—fostered in Deborah a belief that if she was willing to embrace her natural potential, she could grow beyond her humble beginnings.

With the courage to "dream big," she went on to graduate from Barnard College of Columbia University. Then, fueled by her own healthy sense of "I can do this," she started up her own business. Umbrellas Plus, a multimillion-dollar enterprise in New Jersey that designs and markets custom and private-label leisure furniture, sun accessories, and rain products for corporate promotions and retailers, is the product of Deborah's belief in her own special worth.

In a recent speech, she declared, "You are the only one of you in the history of time. For a long time, I was ashamed of who I was and where I came from. Now, I've learned that my greatest power comes from celebrating my uniqueness."

That speech, by the way, was given to a group of women in the ballroom of the very same hotel where her grandmother once scrubbed floors!

A fifty-something-year-old entrepreneur in New Mexico tells another case in point. She decided to embrace her authenticity in what might seem like a more trivial way but nonetheless, for her, was symbolic. Reyna, who had dyed her hair for years, decided to let it grow out "natural." As an operator of a wellness center, she counsels her patients to be true to themselves. Obviously, her personal decision related to what she felt was her professional message. She says that since she's "gone gray," it seems her patients follow her advice with much more regard.

I asked her if she felt that those of us who give nature a little help with a highlight or two were being untrue to ourselves. Her answer: "The beauty of that question is that there's only one woman who can answer it. How comfortable we feel inside ourselves, only we know. And for most women, it has nothing to do with the color of their hair."

Reyna did what felt right for her. She listened to and honored that little voice inside of her that told her it was time to celebrate the accumulation of her years of experience and wisdom. She acted on it—in her own behalf. We've all heard the comment, "She's different on the inside." Don't let this be a description of you.

Self-confidence comes from that cry inside that says, "I believe in me." Your willingness to embrace the unique woman that you are and trust—as well as to act on—your potential is your greatest source for success.

What Have You Done for Me (Yourself) Lately?

Another crutch on which we rely besides copycat behavior is what we've been or what we've accomplished in the past. Yesterday's achievements become a model for what we can be. When your self-confidence is based *only* on past experiences however, it won't carry you well into the unknown future. "I can't do this because I've never done it before" becomes your rationale.

And a low self-esteem craves familiarity, which may feel comfortable, but doing the same things over and over suffocates the passion in life, leaving behind a mechanical existence. Your growth is stunted if you derive your self-confidence from any other source other than your willingness to take on new things. "I trust myself to be able to do that" is the kind of thinking where your greatest potential lies.

For women who are bucking tradition—especially those entering into male-dominated arenas—a sturdy self-esteem is not an option. And those struggles, which come with the territory, quench the thirst for challenges that a woman with a healthy self-esteem is inclined to have. It's a perpetual cycle: a high self-esteem feeds itself with ambition and a willingness to embrace the unknown, which in turn raises our self-esteem. Stretching outside of our comfort zone is a cause *and* effect of a strong self-esteem.

Selling yourself, presenting the real you for others to see, is not complicated. Be yourself. Don't borrow someone else's act (or in my case, clothes). Give yourself permission to try new things. Trust yourself. Self-confidence comes from being comfortable with the person you know you can be—not who you're pretending to be or not the same you that you've always been. Being true to yourself is the first marker on the road to a healthy self-esteem.

Practice Awareness

By dropping—rather than polishing—your act, you'll unleash your very own personal power. You'll bask in permission where once you felt restriction. It's like a wake-up experience for your mind and spirit. Once your life begins to reflect who you really are, you'll find yourself living in the present tense. Living with awareness brings illumination to our lives. We begin to notice things. When we show up in our lives—really show up—we start seeing the possibilities.

A female executive who travels extensively for her business says that the transformation that came about when she decided to live her life in the here and now was like a "clearing of the clouds."

Where once she'd make her way through busy airports with a cell phone glued to her ear, now she pauses to see babies with chubby cheeks in strollers. She smiles at them and they smile back. When at one time she'd rush past an elderly couple clinging to each other for the courage to maneuver through the intimidating hustle-and-bustle of an airport terminal, now she stops and helps them find their way. Their gratitude is the stuff good days are made of—and we're all worthy of good stuff.

While the possibilities that surface from living consciously may seem small at first, we should recognize that covering every minute of every day with busy-bee activities is a way of hiding. It's a mask for insecurities. In an attempt to seek approval from others, we are, in essence, attempting to fool them into thinking that we're worthwhile people. And while we may succeed in fooling the world, we become invisible to ourselves.

Living a life with awareness allows us to listen actively to ourselves. "I don't have time to find myself," says an English teacher with two children. "Between my students and my own kids, most of the time I can't even hear myself think." Too many of us can identify with her predicament. Our self-value is diminished when we can't experience ourselves fully. Since intuition is enhanced with listening and creativity is an offspring of intuition, it follows that when we're not able to hear our inner desires, we're bound to feel lifeless—and worthless.

Another self-esteem toxin is the numbing effect brought on by immersing ourselves in routine tasks. This behavior robs us of the chance to learn and increase our competence and confidence. We're not being true to ourselves when we go through life like robots.

It's only when we live with a heightened sense of awareness that we are open for opportunities. "Sometimes I feel that I'm just putting in my time," says a female mid-level manager. This kind of thinking, while sad, might work for someone inside the big corporate scene, but it won't work for a woman desiring to go out on her own. Entrepreneurship is not a prison sentence. Nor is it for those who view life as a passionless place to exist.

Living your life in the present tense cultivates a self-appreciation, which is an essential component for a thriving self-esteem. The payoff comes when you start realizing how simple life's pleasures are and how deserving you are of them. Whether you're simply giving a baby something to smile about or giving an elderly person some kind of enlightenment, you'll feel a boost in your self-value.

Appreciate Yourself

When you develop a healthy appreciation of yourself, your need for it from other people is diminished. If your motive for pleasing others is strictly to gain their love and acceptance, you leave yourself vulnerable to negative feelings when you fail to please them. You're apt to feel a sense of guilt and shame, emotions that cannot coexist with a healthy self-esteem.

Just ask Terri Bowersock, who as a child was labeled "lazy and dumb as a cue ball" by her teachers and voted Least Likely to Succeed by her peers. Terri suffered from dyslexia.

Now in her mid-forties, she recalls how in the third grade, when she was called on to read out loud, she would turn into the class clown so that she'd be kicked out to the hallway. Those were days when she felt like a "worthless failure."

As time went on, she realized that she needed to come up with her own measure of her self. She knew that while she might not have measured up to the other kids academically, she did have other talents and abilities on which she could rely. For example, she had a way of talking to people that made them listen. She also discovered an "artsy" side she liked about herself.

By the time she became an adult, she had learned to appreciate her own unique strengths. Refusing to be held back by the disbelief of others, she decided to go out on her own. Her well-developed charm and her dogged determination paved the way.

She began by spreading the word; "Bring me what you need to get rid of and I'll sell it for you." That was the beginning of Terri's New and Consigned Furnishings. Her sixteen-store chain is currently valued at over $26 million! Her self-value? Priceless.

Because Terri believed that she had the power to determine her own worth, she was able to tap into a reservoir of strengths, namely a passion to inspire others who suffer from dyslexia. Her favorite cause, as you might guess, one to which she gives much of her time and many of her resources, is the International Dyslexia Association. As a public speaker her message is: "No one can *be* a failure; failure is an event."

There's an irony to her story. As a girl, her work earned her big red marks scrawled across her paper. As a woman, she's earned high marks, being named an Avon Women of Enterprise honoree and One of the Hottest Entrepreneurs in America according to *Inc.* magazine.

When we accept, appreciate, and love ourselves, failure becomes something we're willing to risk because it comes with no associated guilt. Our motive for doing something is for our own sake. That's quite different from needing the acceptance of other people where a failure invites guilt. Almost all legendary people have learned to give themselves permission to risk failure. This means doing things for the joy of doing them, not for how much praise you can garner.

Billie Jean King, who dominated women's tennis for more

than twenty-five years, practiced her sport according to her often-quoted philosophy: "Be bold. If you're going to make an error, make a doozy, and don't be afraid to hit the ball." She never let anything get in her way of her desire to "hit the ball"—including such long-standing handicaps as bad eyesight, difficulties with breathing, and chronic knee pain. To Billie Jean, failure was a passing event. It did not define who she was.

Another legend, jazz singer Ella Fitzgerald, had an instinctive approach when it came to making failure her friend. As a girl, she had always dreamed of becoming a dancer. She would perform on street corners in Yonkers, New York, where the passersby would applaud her with small change. In her teens, she entered an amateur talent contest at the Apollo Theater in Harlem intending, of course, to dance. Instead, she was paralyzed by stage fright. She failed to move. So what did she do? She began singing! She won the $25 prize money that night and went on to become a legendary singer, recording over 250 albums.

Showing appreciation to someone is always an act of kindness. Giving it to yourself is an act of responsibility. What you're actually appreciating is your potential, which is the source of self-confidence. While it doesn't inoculate you from failure, it gives you the ability to bounce back from it. Self-appreciation nurtures your self-esteem so you're not constantly seeking to make someone feel a certain way about you. Therefore, you're less apt to struggle from a sense of letting them down.

Forgive Yourself

As we women move away from our traditionally assigned and exclusively designated role as caregivers, we are faced with the challenge of forgiving ourselves for not living up to the expectations of others. A healthy self-esteem cannot be nurtured in a climate of inner turmoil.

In a recently published article, I was quoted as saying that my sons ate a lot of TV dinners when they were growing up, because I was working long hours (that was until they learned to cook). That comment generated calls, cards, and letters, mostly from mothers all over the country dealing with maternal guilt.

In the course of writing this book, I talked with hundreds of women (entrepreneurs, corporate women, and homemakers) about the toughest issues facing them at home and in business. Across the board, they listed "maternal guilt" in the top two! "I should have baked more cookies," or "I should have attended more soccer games," is the way many of them put it.

The truth is, mothers are getting more than their share of blame. From criminal behavior amongst teens to the lack of stable home lives, society is tough on moms. But after struggling to understand this issue in my own mind, I realized that by blaming society for my guilt, I was giving up my own personal power. I was powerless to rid myself of my shame. When we're dependent on the approval of others to make us feel valued, we inevitably set ourselves up to feel guilty. And when we blame others for our guilt, we render ourselves powerless.

Early in my career, after hearing me beat myself up one day, my younger son sat me down and said, "Mom, you're a good enough mom." He claims that my career really took off after that. But the real acquittal came when I said those words to myself: "I'm a good enough mom." By doing so, I forgave myself for my past shortcomings as a mother. I knew that whatever mistakes I'd made, I did the best I could with the information and experience I had at the time.

Try telling yourself that you're a "good enough" mom, or wife, or sister, or daughter. It's liberating. When we forgive ourselves, we make room in our lives to be the best that we can be now—in the present. And as long as you deny yourself forgiveness for who you were or what you did, you linger in internal conflict and your self-esteem is the casualty.

From early childhood, women have been programmed to sacrifice themselves—their wants and needs—to others. The answer to every request for our time, energy, whatever has to be yes. We have a need to win the favor of others. Our aim is acceptance. In the pursuit of it, we engage in self-rejection.

It's not surprising that so many of the women's magazines today feature articles on the art of saying no. The one most common conclusion coming from all of these articles is that women take too long to say no. Our "no" comes off as an apology because of our desire for approval, usually from the person doing the asking.

I learned how to say "no" from Mike, my executive assistant, who coordinates my calendar. In the past, whenever I'd have to decline an invitation, I'd give him blow-by-blow instructions as to how to respond: "Make sure they fully understand why I'm declining, Mike. Make sure you tell them blah, blah, blah."

One day I overheard him on the phone saying, "Ms. Brem won't be able to speak to your group next month. She has a scheduling conflict." That was it! That was a far cry from what I had told him to say; I told him to tell them where I was traveling, for what purpose, as well as what flight I'd be taking. After I voiced my objections to his handling of the call, he defended himself. "Marion, I've been doing it this way for years and the invitations keep coming."

Here he had been running my office all of this time the guy way—you know, the way men seem to keep words to a minimum. He taught me a great life lesson. The best way to say "no" is what I call "Mike's Way." Keep it short and sweet. Ladies, I promise you—the invitations will keep coming.

Self-forgiveness is the best way to win the war with yourself. Self-acceptance is the result, which is an essential building block of strong self-esteem.

If I make a case that women have an innately different

business style than men—okay, better in many regards—then, I have to be prepared to answer why women have not made even greater progress. And while I do not deny the existence of many gender inequities in our society, I do believe that one of the greatest obstacles holding women back is the low value we tend to put on ourselves. I believe this is good news because we have the power to fix it.

Women and men have primary ways in which each self-identifies: men by their jobs, women by their relationships. Self-esteem, for both sexes, is directly linked to how we see ourselves. The problem with identifying ourselves through relationships is that we relinquish much of our own personal power. We rely too heavily on the approval of others. We have trouble accepting praise and we make self-defeating comparisons.

With a healthy self-esteem, we're well equipped and energized to pursue our dreams. And we're better able to enjoy the pleasures of life. A belief in our ability to take care of our own needs comes from a willingness to be true to ourselves. Embracing our authenticity wakes us up to opportunities that fit us uniquely. Appreciating and forgiving ourselves gives us the freedom to bring our own sensitivities into the business world.

nine

Sensitivity

Heather Jenkins credits her "female sensitivity" for her success as an owner of a home accessory store. She has a way of anticipating her customer's wishes and whims, which she is always happy to accommodate. The more difficult the challenge, the more pride she feels in delivering.

But perhaps her same "female sensitivity" is the reason she found it tough to accept a rejection from her banker for a loan extension. Feeling violated, she allowed the rejection to get the best of her. With her energy zapped, she became sullen and withdrawn—even cold. Her business suffered over subsequent weeks, more from her bruised feelings than from the financial consequence of the banker's decision.

To find a good balance between being sensitive and overly sensitive, it is important to understand the roots of our feelings. And with the continuing authority of demeaning stereotypes, it is equally important to recognize and respect gender differences as they relate to sensitivities at work.

Being sensitive allows women to be thoughtful and responsive, but being overly sensitive makes a woman a slave to the opinions and needs of others. Creativity is the first casualty of hurt feelings. And a woman relinquishes other powers—such as the ability to rebound from problems sensibly and seek alternative solutions—when she allows her feelings to rule her world.

Finding the balance between being a woman who can bring warm sensitivity to the business world and being a woman who is out of control with her feelings is a challenging assignment. But it is not impossible. Seeing clearly that most criticisms and rejections are not personal (even though they may appear to be) is the first step. Accepting constructive criticism and rejection—without blame—is the stuff learning is made of. Second, possessing and using our spirit of forgiveness will help us avoid the pitfall of the hurt.

I have learned in my conquest for new zones of achievement in business (and in life for that matter) to avoid the sabotage of self-defeating, emotionally charged behavior, all the time remaining true to my womanhood. It can be done.

The Root of Our Feelings

"You really make me angry," a parent tells a child. I bet you heard something of the sort time and time again when you were growing up. Most children do. It's understandable why you might have come to assume that you're responsible for other people's feelings. Then, by extension, they must be responsible for yours. When you blame others for what you feel and blame yourself for what others feel, you're in effect scrambling the signals that act as an interpreter for your beliefs.

Bobbi Sims, creator of a popular video series, *From Ordinary to Extraordinary*, says, "Once we understand that feelings are a sensory response to thinking and the concept penetrates our unconscious mind, we can begin to experience our feelings without judgment." What I hear—or should I say feel—in that message is that feelings are useful, as long as we recognize them for what they are, messages to let us know what's going on out there. Ms. Sims adds, "We can learn to feel our feelings and control our behavior."

If you've suffered a great personal loss, you're familiar with the grief and pain that follows. You probably hurt everywhere. The message your feeling of pain sent you was that you cared. Your feelings were an indicator that all was right with your system. But the way we feel emotionally need not rule our behavior.

As women, we *do* have big feelings. Our emotional nature is part of our uniqueness. After all, our capacity to love is only as great as our capacity to feel. Think of the many people today (many, many men) who are commitment-phobic and afraid to feel for fear of hurt. They're not running their lives; they're running from them, for a willingness to love is a willingness to hurt.

At the other extreme are the people we know who keep reliving the pain that prevents the healing. They act as though forgiving—whether it's themselves or someone else— will set them up for future pain. For them, forgiveness is right up there with letting their guard down. The truth is that when hurt is allowed to heal, it sometimes leaves scars. But I often say that my scars are my stars, providing the light that guides me but doesn't control me.

It has occurred to me that these types of discussions regarding feelings rooted in childhood and stifled by fear and ignorance have not been commonly upheld in the dimensions of previous business books. But I believe the arrival of female ambitions on the business scene has opened up communication rich with possibility for cultural change.

Vive la Différence

I was recently reminded of the work of psychiatrist and author Mark Goulston, who says that in his couples' therapy, the solutions he offers have to *make sense* to men and *feel right* to women. That is, he appeals to a man's reason and a woman's emotions.

Feelings, like intuition, are an important way for women to interact with the world. After all, passion, which drives us, is an intense conviction or overmastering feeling. But the truth is that men don't want to be objects of our emotion, especially in the business world. I am not advocating that women stifle their feelings (or act like a man). But I do believe that a continued indictment of our patriarchal business climate—in lieu of a willingness to look in the mirror— will not serve to empower women in careers.

Yes, I cringe when I open letters that read "Dear Mr. Brem." I feel the offense that comes from recognizing that the pronoun "she" has never stood for both sexes. I know that equal rights for men have never had to inspire a march, let alone a constitutional amendment. I acknowledge that any woman of success is more apt to be accepted if she is viewed as typically feminine. That is, nonaggressive, nonconfrontational, but rather sweet and nice.

Even the language commonly used in business reflects

and expresses primarily male experiences and values. I've considered the many phrases taken from sports and the military: ballpark estimate, home run, team player, starting line up, touchdown, over the fence, eye on the ball, battle strategy, bull's-eye, launch a campaign, big guns, under the gun, plan of attack, and the list goes on.

But in the end, the universe of discourse that prevails shapes the people that participate in the discourse. And both sexes are now participating.

In my experience in fitting into a community with men—and even leading them—it has become important for me to understand the downside of my otherwise wonderful trait—sensitivity.

Self-Defeating Behaviors

Remember no one can make you feel
inferior without your consent.
—ELEANOR ROOSEVELT

Sensitivity can be valuable when it's tempered with sound reason. When it's not, it can get in our way. I know for a fact that oversensitivity plagues women in the workplace and is the primary cause of ridicule and exclusion.

A woman's ability to command the respect necessary to build collaborations and to lead others becomes compromised when she personalizes business issues. Other people's actions are a statement about them, not about you. And when you take things personally, you empower the other party.

A good way to think of inappropriately expressed feelings in the workplace is what I call the hot-stove principle. If you place your hand on a hot stove, you get burned. The burn causes pain, which is a signal telling you to remove your hand. Your response prevents further injury. You then treat it to aid its healing. But if you take offense to the stove—maybe by hitting it—you're acting out your pain in a way that is nonproductive, even to the extent of adding insult to injury. And if your pain is harbored to the extent that you never turn the stove on again, you've allowed it to overpower you.

The hot-stove principle allows you to feel the feelings and take them seriously but not personally.

Judith, a young partner in a law firm, learned this principle about self-defeating behavior with one of her first cases. Charged with preparing the case in a very short time, as was her custom, she met the challenge. Proud of her seemingly impossible accomplishment, she anxiously awaited her managing partner's response to her delineated strategies. She felt crushed when he labeled the file "a complete misfire." She thought about the time she'd put into the work. She thought about all of the other lawyers she'd run it by and how they had praised it.

The criticism hurt her so badly that she became paralyzed to rework the case. The clock kept ticking. The dead-line drew nearer. The managing partner called her to ask how she was coming along. She seized the opportunity to tell him how he had hurt her feelings. His response was one you might guess: Too bad, so sad, we have a deadline here. He then told her that he felt compelled to give the case to some-one else. Barely disguising her anger, she insisted on one more chance and he relented. At that moment, she decided that while her feelings were very real to her, they were not going to dictate her actions. She prepared and submitted a second strategy, this time to only light criticism from him but praises from the jury.

What this experience taught Judith was that when she wallowed in her hurt, she interrupted her ability to create, to produce, and to move past the hurt. Her feeling of rejection was there only to tell her how much she cared about her new position in the firm and the case. When she internalized the feeling, she empowered it beyond its intended purpose. She also gave her partner power—not only over the case but also over her day.

Being ultrasensitive and allowing emotions to take over causes us to lose sight of our objectives—business or other-wise. Like Judith, I didn't learn this from a book. Less than one year into my first sales job, I thought I pretty much had it all figured out. Feeling like I was more sensitive than my male counterparts to my customer's wants and needs (espe-cially the female customers), I thought I had all the edge I

would ever need. For instance, take the way most of the salesmen would focus their attention on the male halves of couples.
To me, that made them insensitive. By contrast, I catered to
the women. "The key to my sales success has been the keen
attention I pay to my female customers," reads one of my
quotes in a trade publication.

One punishing August afternoon, I picked up a sales call
that was to humble me into a personal re-evaluation. The
woman on the other end of the line poured out her tale of woe
to me. She described herself as a recent divorcée and a victim
of domestic violence with no credit. She had a new job that
she was to start the following week but her broken-down car
wouldn't even make it out of her driveway. Visions of my own
not-too-distant-past experiences in desperate circumstances
came vividly to mind and I immediately leaped to her aid. I
got directions to her home so that I could be her chauffeur—
and new best friend—for the long bumper-to-bumper drive
back to the dealership.

Back at the showroom it didn't take long to find the right
car for her and the long consultation working through the
issues of credit and financing immediately gave her a sense of
control over her life. Much later that night, after I took her
home, I fell into bed feeling good about the service I had
given this damsel in distress.

The next afternoon, I picked her up as planned and we
proceeded to the dealership to pick up her very first new car.
She got out of my car and walked over to the car she had

selected the night before. She turned to me and said, "I've changed my mind."

"What? You've got to be kidding!" I was flabbergasted.

"I think I've rushed into this," she responded somewhat defensively. "I want to talk it over with my ex-husband."

Almost speechless, I managed to blurt out something about being embarrassed for my gender today and then strode back to the showroom. How could this lady do this to herself—and to me? I had jumped through hoops for her. She owed me more consideration.

My manager made arrangements to take the customer home and then called me into his office. I was still steaming.

"You've taken this way too personally," he declared.

"You're acting like what happened here today is my fault," I responded in exasperation, my voice going up at least half an octave.

"Marion, it's not a matter of blame, or who did what to whom. It's what *didn't* happen here that concerns me. We lost a sale today. And worse, you got way too emotionally involved with the customer and pretty well killed any chance that she'll come back when she's ready to buy."

His words stung but he was right. To this day they have left their permanent imprint on me.

Our feelings are meant to be an internal guide, there to interpret what's going on externally: In my case, I had grown to care about this woman. I was feeling pride in my ability to help another woman empower herself. And of course, I also cared about making the sale. Yet, I would have been better off had I honored my feelings in such a way that didn't allow them to be the CEO of my day.

In a relationship, if someone has the capability to hurt you, you know you care for them. The same is true in business. If you truly don't ever feel hurt, you're in the wrong business. You feel good when a client calls you and asks you to double his order. You feel hurt when a client calls you to cancel or doesn't place an order in the first place. It's painful when your competitor boxes you out or when the bank turns your loan down. It's impossible to care about getting the business and not care about losing it. If you should ever become so callous that losing business is no big deal, face it: It's quitting time.

The question is what are you supposed to do with the hurt? What part should feelings play in the game of business?

During my early professional life, I felt sustained by my ability to nurture others. But I was still letting my feelings govern my actions above common sense. If I felt offended by one of my colleague's criticisms, I would say to myself, "I'll show him." Although I was maturing, my universe was still very centered on other people's opinions of me.

I recall how hurt I felt when a female executive with my parent company called to share some things with me, as she put it, "for your own good." After I courageously gave her a green light to proceed, she told me that my reputation for being too sensitive was hurting me "with the guys."

She offered examples of times when I had been left out

of the loop because people feared my emotional reaction. As she put it: "The men are afraid to say 'Boo' to you." Ouch! Because I am ultrasensitive, her comment pierced me through the heart.

I can't fully explain why, but I continued listening to her (and with no tears). She had touched a hot button. Who wants to be left out? I somehow gracefully managed to end the conversation and we hung up.

For a long time I thought about her words, imagining how my colleagues must have talked about me behind my back. I created scenarios in which they ridiculed and avoided me. This was not paranoia. This was the truth. She had provided me with the evidence. Though I felt deeply hurt by what she had told me, I was not harmed. And I never made any attempt to deny myself the feelings. I knew that my feelings never lie to me. Rather, my feelings were telling me that something had to change and the change had to begin with me!

For starters, I had to create ways to engage in some damage control. I made phone calls. I arranged meetings. I put a new me on display for all to see. That's what entrepreneurs do. They make changes that sometimes involve reinventing themselves. This time I wasn't going to let my emotions run away from me or with me. It's true. She had helped me realize that being an emotional hemophiliac had been detrimental to my business.

Positive changes did start taking place that never could have or would have, had I denied myself the time and space to feel. It was wise, too, that I had chosen not to blow up at her or otherwise get defensive. It was critical that I did not assume or assign blame. I look back on our conversation and my reaction to it and I realize that it marked a real turning point in my business life. Though I hadn't invited this lesson, I'm grateful to have learned so much from it.

Who's to Blame?

Management consultant Dr. Adele Scheele, who received her Ph.D. from UCLA as a Change Management Fellow, says that women play a "blame game" with themselves. We automatically assume that when something goes wrong, we must be to blame. Sometimes a negative response—feeling bad and suffering hurt—is natural. But self-blame is not the most constructive interpretation of events. Believe it or not, there are factors at play that are not about you.

At a workshop I conducted for Latinas on the Move in San Jose on the topic of "Failure Is Never Final," an entry-level manager employed in a retail outlet posed a very good question. Having just been denied a promotion, she stated that she felt like she was to blame for the outcome. "If I'm supposed to learn from my failures, don't I need to accept full responsibility for them?" she asked.

Sure, we know that failures are events that always have a lesson in them. But getting passed over for a promotion is not necessarily a failure. I reminded her that she might have done everything right. Her boss may have used bad judgment or there may, in fact, have been someone more appropriate for the particular job.

Rosa Defa, executive director for the Executive Women International Corporate Offices, has an interesting perspective on why women have a tendency to take things personally. She points out that women have a "committed desire to find solutions when something goes wrong." She believes that women look internally *first* for the answer. That doesn't mean they necessarily stay there. Women ask themselves questions such as "What did I do wrong? Did I play a part in this mishap?" Because women internalize experiences and personalize their commitments they are more vulnerable to hurt.

Because men tend to take things less personally, they process information externally. They attack a problem by reaching out for a solution. Men ask themselves questions such as "What is wrong here? What's it going to take to fix this?" They take on a business challenge pointing their finger out, not in.

When something falls apart or doesn't go as planned, recognize that there are outside forces at play. Conversely, when things go well—even better than expected—you may need to settle down and realize that outside factors play a part in successes too.

Handling Criticism and Rejection

Jack and Maureen were both candidates for a promotion at a national surgical equipment and supply company. Jack was promoted over Maureen because, in the words of their boss, "Jack is better at taking criticism."

Though Maureen had demonstrated a high level of competency, on at least a few occasions she had left the office citing "stress." By her own admission, it wasn't the workload associated with her job that stressed her out; it was the people. She eventually developed a reputation among her peers (and boss) of being someone who went around wearing her heart on her sleeve.

Maureen's response to the decision betrayed her emotional vulnerability: "How dare they think that I can't take criticism?" she complained.

The ability to accept criticism graciously is important to your career development for two reasons. First, if people feel that you are too easily offended, they're likely to withhold potentially useful information from you. Second, when you resist constructive criticism, you put the other party on the defensive, causing them to turn up the volume of their criticisms.

I am by no means suggesting that you should subject yourself to constant, unconstructive criticism. That's not criticism. That's verbal abuse. But being too *touchy* is going to

leave you feeling ignored and isolated. Accepting constructive criticism for what it is—an offer to help you do better—
will go a long way to enforcing your role as a team player.

Sometimes being the object of criticism is simply a matter
of timing. Consider Nancy, who owns a real estate company
that specializes in Florida retirement properties catering
mostly to seniors. On one occasion, she had been showing
properties to a retired couple, accompanied by their daughter.
For several hours she could sense the husband's mood deteri-
orating. Finally, in an unexpected outburst he told his wife,
"It's time to find another, more competent realtor."

Nancy was crushed. She even called in sick for two days,
staying home to lick her wounds. The self-doubt she experienced incapacitated her to the point where she couldn't even
get dressed. Then the phone rang. It was the couple's daughter calling to apologize and explain that her dad was doing
much better now after his "bout." His "bout," it turn out, was
a diabetic episode for which he was taken to the hospital that
same day! With his condition now stabilized, they wanted to
revisit one of the properties.

Though she ended up closing the transaction, the real
payoff was the lesson she learned: Sometimes we step right
smack into the firing line of someone's wrath simply because
we're in the wrong place at the wrong time.

Along the road of criticism we meet rejection. That is, an
inability to accept constructive criticism is linked to a fear of

rejection. When we're overly sensitive, we resist helpful criticism. And from this behavior we sometimes unwittingly invite the very rejection we fear. In doing so, we actually block our own advancements.

Tonya, a mid-level manager at an oil refinery, has trained many men who went on to higher executive positions. Though somewhat frustrated by this pattern, she has always chosen to accept her situation because she's never wanted to risk losing their acceptance.

One of the men who was trained by Tonya, along with his wife, became a personal friend of hers. One night at a party at their home, Tonya found herself alone with the wife. In the kitchen, replenishing the hors d'oeuvres trays, the wife told Tonya that her husband considered her to be overqualified for her position, but he had never promoted her, because she had "never asked" to be.

When Tonya told me of her experience, she acknowledged that her fear of rejection had been so severe that she never wanted to risk asking for what she was rightfully due. Her situation is not an unusual one for many women in business. As we've seen in the previous chapter on self-esteem, asking for what you feel you deserve does not come easily to most of us. In fact, even when we finally overcome our initial fear of rejection, it's not uncommon to hear our requests covered in so many qualifiers—maybe's or but's—that it can result in precisely the reaction we'd feared. We become so apologetic in our requests for a raise, a promotion, or any sign of recognition of our worth that we still don't get what we want or deserve.

The Power of No

But let's say you faced your fears and asked someone to accept your idea. With no apologies, you managed to hold your head up high with the sound of confidence in your voice.

You asked your sister to host Thanksgiving dinner at *her* home this year. You asked your husband to extend his vacation. You asked your boyfriend for a commitment. You asked your prospect to buy your product or service. The answer you get is "No." What next?

One of my salesmen has a coffee mug that reads, "The sale begins with the word 'No.' " He has it on his desk even when he's not drinking coffee. He tells me that his mug has actually earned him much business. He claims that when a customer does say "No," he smiles and looks at the cup and it usually causes a chuckle. He and the customers recognize that "No" means only not now or not this way or not this one. "No" is not a personal rejection.

"No" can be a great teacher. It can guide you to better rephrase a question for the future. It can show you how to lay more solid groundwork for the request. It can reveal much about your customer and it can reveal a lot about you.

Barbara, one remarkable fund-raiser I know, keeps a "No" book. Her "Turn Downs" become the basis for future follow-up. With each rejection, she tracks industry trends and other details that help her know more about her prospects. She has determined, for example, that large corporations tend to make their commitments for the following year during September when they set their budgets. Waiting until January to ask for money put her organization out of consideration. Without the initial rejection, she wouldn't have learned this. With the help of her "No" book, she was able to double her fund-raising efforts from one year to the next.

Forgive and Move On

At some point in our lives we all are disappointed or hurt by someone else. It takes great courage to resist the temptation to stay hurt. The truth is when we decide to have courage to forgive others we then define our goal. We know the place we want to get to. The decision to have courage also gives us the support we'll need for the journey.

As I write this, I'm thinking of a lady who came up to me after a speech on forgiveness that I gave in San Francisco. She confessed that she had found it difficult but possible to forgive people in her life seeking forgiveness, but did not know how to forgive someone who wasn't asking for, or even wanting, forgiveness.

She went on to share with me that she was three years out from a very painful divorce. Since the divorce, she had lost her job, many friends, her ability to sleep, and her self-esteem. In fact, the only thing she'd gained was too much weight. "I can't seem to get it together," she said.

As she went on, I could tell that clearly the woman was in pain. I suggested to her that she seek professional counseling (which she later did) but in the meantime, it would probably provide her some relief if she could get her feelings out by writing them down on a sheet of paper.

Later, she sent me a note to tell me that she had taken my advice—only this task had taken sixteen (!) sheets of paper to accomplish. She credited the act of "journaling" her feelings with turning her life around. It had created for her a flow of forgiveness, even toward someone that had no interest in receiving it. She gradually came to recognize how much hold her ex-husband, the divorce—the whole ordeal—had had on her.

Her pain was real but she finally let it go—for her own sake!

Drawing on my experience working in a male-dominated work culture, I have learned that the sensitivity that women bring to business is a good thing. I have enjoyed many successes because I dared to show my sensitive side. But I have also learned to temper my emotions with calm reason. To do this, I have had to acknowledge that taking things personally makes us vulnerable. In essence, we forfeit our personal power when we give someone else permission to hurt us via our feelings.

Once we accept that everything is not always about us, once we recognize that external forces are always at work, we're better able to feel our feelings but control our behavior. When we internalize events such as failures, we risk losing our head when we need it most.

Criticism and rejection have been my best teachers, although I haven't always been the best student. And when everything else fails and I feel compelled to blame myself— or others—for ridicule or exclusion, which I might suffer, I am quick to forgive. After all, I know that our strengths cannot flourish if our vulnerabilities undermine our self-worth.

Part 4

No book about business or entrepreneurism would be complete without a discussion of leadership. In fact, common wisdom tells us that in the corporate world leadership is the key to making an organization function successfully. It's clear, or at least I hope that I've made the point throughout this book, that the qualities with which women are innately endowed make them good leaders.

There are countless volumes devoted to leadership, many of which call up some of those very qualities—passion, resiliency, creativity—that I have specifically attributed to women. And it is the development of these qualities that authors of these books seek to encourage in their traditionally male readers. But what most of the other books do not do is examine the fundamental differences in the way men and women approach their careers. Generally speaking, as women seek to gain more control over their professional lives—as they move up the corporate ladder or start their own businesses—they have never been able to leave behind the traditionally female responsibilities of home and family. Therefore, they have had to draw more deeply on their strengths or shore up their weakness more securely to be able to tackle the tasks at hand. In order to function in *all* aspects of their lives, they have had to bring an important element to leadership—a sense of balance—which men, for the most part, have not had to consider.

There is no equivalent for the term "mommy track" for men. Mr. Mom is still an anomaly. It is still almost universally assumed that women will continue to be the primary care-givers, certainly for the children but also for their husbands, and increasingly for their own parents. These are the realities of modern life and modern business. And so too is the reality that success for most women requires a new definition.

Without ignoring the bottom line, the corner office, or the six-figure salary, the truth is that women can find balance in their lives that allows them to attain personal and profes-sional satisfaction by anyone's measure. And the best place to do this is with their own businesses. Women still need to understand the importance of effective leadership. They must learn to appreciate that they can be decision-makers, the primary role of leaders, even though they have the rep for being indecisive creatures.

In light of the female strengths with which we have become acquainted, it is evident that considering the importance of leadership and balance *together* will define the meaning of true success.

ten

Leadership

I f I change my mind a million times, I want to hear him say, 'I like it that way.' " Those are the lyrics from one of my favorite country songs, "Any Man of Mine," sung passionately by Shania Twain. The stereotype of women being indecisive has not been a subject of many debates. After all, it's a "woman's prerogative" to be able to change her mind. How, then, can a woman be a good leader, charged with making decisions, when she's considered to be—and even takes pride in being—indecisive?

Leadership is the key to running a good business. And

making decisions is the primary responsibility of a leader. Therefore, it's clear that it's time for us, as women, to make an adjustment in the way we view and project ourselves. There's nothing cute about being fickle in business. This may be an unromantic way of looking at it but to be a good decision-maker, a woman has got to project confidence and resist swaying to satisfy the opinions of others. My sweet intuition and sometimes not-so-sweet experience has revealed to me that only when my sensitivities have been in check and my self-esteem has been in good health have I been an effective leader.

The first decision any of us makes as a leader is to determine the purpose of why we're doing what we do. Passion is the fire that creates meaning for everything in our lives—including what our business can and will do. Whether it's making pottery or delivering stellar customer service, our epiphany comes when we're able to say, "This is it!"

Next, we've got to be able to define the means of getting the job done. It takes a lot of nurturing to make what's interesting to us and what's useful to others come together. Flexibility and resiliency become coping mechanisms to keep our creativity alive so that we're able to embrace new ways to approach the challenges and to overcome setbacks.

Finally, and in my opinion the most engaging aspect of leadership, is the job of motivating other players. Sharing your passion with employees and nurturing their talents through appreciation, development, and discipline will give you the most valuable return on your investment of time and money. As hard as it may be to imagine, sometimes people *want* to join together for some vision. And humans teach other humans what to do. Your role as a leader is to show them how. It's the most powerful interaction in our universe.

Once a leader has determined her purpose and defined the means with which to pull it off, she's poised to shape her own environment. The result is change. Fearless leaders create change in the face of sometimes nagging uncertainty.

And while leadership appears to come more easily to some people, there is no identifiable gene that makes one person more adept at leadership than another. It is certainly not a gender issue, although history might indicate otherwise. I know. I discovered that while I may have had an innate talent for leadership, the skills of leadership needed serious nurturing. But luckily, early on in my CEOship, I embraced my strengths and used them to reinvent the way I did business.

Growing into Leadership

As the oldest of five children, I assumed many leadership functions early in life. I was the "big sister" that fixed problems for my siblings and sometimes still do. To be honest, I've enjoyed the role of family fixer and leader.

Growing up, I would lead family Christmas plays, casting and directing my three brothers and one sister. I used bribery, blackmail, whatever I had to do—all in the name of holiday spirit. I suppose my passion for creating an entertaining homespun production was contagious. And so, they joined in.

When I started my own business, I thought I was carrying a lifetime of training in leadership. It had begun with my "big sister" experiences. And because people are infinitely interesting to me, sales proved to be the perfect place for the development of my people skills. Similarly, my experience as a finance manager honed my expertise in money management. At the time, I was confident that I was ready to lead my own team.

At first, with only seven employees all reporting to me, life was wonderful. Most days we even ate our meals together. We were such a good team that success came early. Then, I blinked and in less than two years seven employees had turned into seventy. It was then that I learned how much of a leader I *wasn't*.

The rapid expansion of the business created a whole new set of problems for which I was not prepared. I had that sinking feeling that left me asking myself, "Did I get in over my head?"

What had gone wrong? I was still doing things the same as I always had. I was still putting in fourteen-to-sixteen-hour days. I was still holding rah-rah meetings. Only now, they were mostly impromptu sessions held at the water fountain— one employee at a time. I was still talking with most of the customers myself. I was still willing and able to put out the fires. (Why were there so many more of them?) Even though I was basically still doing things the same way, everything had changed.

For starters, my staff no longer seemed as loyal as they once had been. Employee turnover was becoming the norm. And cash was flowing all right—flowing right out the door. My once friendly banker now seemed hostile—all because I was overdrawn. Inventory control was definitely out of control. Who was supposed to order cars? A small detail—how could that one have gotten by me? And receivables? Why weren't people paying me the money they owed me? Don't they like me?

As I attempted to unravel the mystery of the political and technical sides of my business problems, I came to realize that there was much I didn't know about leadership. Putting my business in a kind of cruise-control mode, I reached out for help by enrolling myself in a Harvard Business School executive education program. And just for good measure, I read *What They Don't Teach You at Harvard Business School* on the plane to Boston. Teach me leadership, fast!

I've often said that lucky people are constantly searching in the right places. Well, I'm lucky. I got to learn the lesson early enough. Many business leaders don't. My resiliency had enabled me to tear up my business draft and rewrite it.

I learned that leadership is a function of change. Change doesn't just happen to a leader. A leader makes change happen. Behaving like a victim in the heat of trial, I had been doing more reacting than pro-acting. I had to get over the feeling that hardships were coming *at me* and people were doing things *to me*. What I've since come to know is that a winner cannot reside in the same mind as a whiner.

And with my salesperson's mentality in overdrive, I thought more was better. It's not always the case. I had to learn that unmanaged growth means chaos—not something that my bankers, backers, or employees wanted to experience.

I took a close look at companies that had been forced to board up their windows. I learned that more businesses *grow* broke than *go* broke. I also learned that profit isn't a dirty word. Making money and making people happy can be compatible. But my intensive "disease to please," as Oprah Winfrey calls it, had infected that sense of order. Most of the decisions I had been making were allowed to sway with everyone else's opinions—and not necessarily in the direction of the good of the company.

Determining the Purpose

I've never viewed my leadership role with a sense of entitlement but rather as a sense of responsibility and opportunity. There's a power that comes along with any leadership role that creates both. And while we may gain power by helping others and sometimes even just knowing others, we retain it by achieving results.

The need for a leader requires that there be, at the very least, one follower. And absent a tyrannical state of affairs, followers grant consent to the leader to lead. Because followers are important in the structure of power, there's always a need to achieve results—mutually satisfying results. Without results, any leader's power withers and dies. This is why it's so important to define the desired results up front for all parties involved.

What's the purpose of your business? What is it customers want from you? Intuition surely comes into play in assessing whether there's a market or not and whether your product or service can fulfill the potential market's passions; and creativity plays a major role in the way a product or service is conceived.

And what is it you want from the relationship? What charges you up emotionally about the enterprise? What is it about the venture that's going to turn you on enough every day to get up and do it again? Your passion will carry you through the peaks and valleys.

Melissa, a thirty-seven-year-old assistant manager at a chain restaurant, accepted a promotion to a manager's position, which came up quite suddenly when the manager was seriously injured in a plane crash. Though she hadn't lobbied for the new leadership role, she embraced it readily. For one thing, her compensation package almost doubled. She also knew that she would enjoy the opportunity to mingle more with customers as a full-fledged manager than in her old position. She'd walk around offering complimentary desserts and drinks and fulfilling her passion to please people.

Within twelve weeks, she was demoted and offered her previous assistant manager's position, but in another city! "It's all happened so fast. Where'd I go wrong?" she asked the VP at headquarters. He went on to tell her that she had not delivered the expected results. Though the restaurant's profitability had held steady when compared with previous months, this was the time of year when they had expected significant increases. It was then that she realized that she had never even bothered to ask anything about her employers' expectations. Her power came and went.

To have a real lasting power, a leader needs to deliver what helps other people. Since women are naturally helpful, it would seem that leadership should come naturally. And it can, provided that what pleases customers and what turns the wheels of commerce—profitability—are reconciled.

On the day that I received the National Conference of Christians and Jews Humanitarian Award, an interviewer asked me what I felt was my number-one role as a community leader. I responded by saying that it was to maintain my business's profitability. The reporter seemed surprised; I suppose she thought I would respond by talking about my work with the American Cancer Society or the women's shelter. All of my work is important, but what allows me to give my time and money to these philanthropic enterprises is the profitability of my day job, so to speak. Value-based leadership fulfills a larger purpose than just making money, but one can't lose sight of the fundamental demands of business.

My market is fiercely competitive. Shrinking profit margins are a reality. Misconceptions about profit margins live on. Therein lies the challenge associated with many leadership roles in business. But when the obstacles are overcome and pragmatic results are obtained, you become a magnet for new opportunities. The reward for results is more power. And the more power you have, the more opportunities you'll be exposed to, enabling you to achieve even greater results! But it's a trip that can and will be interrupted anytime you don't deliver results. That's why it's so important to be clear up front about what results are expected of you.

Getting power and keeping power is made up of relationship stuff. That's the reality. That's another reason why more women are becoming entrepreneurs. We get it. True power can't be seized by force. It has to be earned and then nurtured.

"Why did you become an entrepreneur?" I posed that question to hundreds of female business owners. Not once did I hear: "I was interested in a get-rich-quick scheme." Sometimes I'd hear about their discontent at larger corporations. By decamping, they decided to claim their own power. Often, I heard how forced change in their lives cried for a solution and starting a business was just what the doctor ordered—sometimes literally. But mostly, I heard how they really felt they had a better way—a better way of cleaning office complexes, a better way of clearing construction debris, a better way of selling cosmetics.

But not everyone who becomes a leader seeks it out as a professional or personal goal. There are those who have leadership thrust upon them, only to learn that the experience helps them to reclaim a buried part of themselves.

One such admirable lady, who rose to the occasion under seemingly unbearable circumstances, is Lois Benjamin-Bohm, whose husband and three children were killed in a car crash.

Grieving, devastated, and perhaps still in a state of shock, she realized that all that was left in her life to show that she had had a life was Shlepper's, a moving company she and her husband had created together ten years earlier. Though she had been part of the team, it was her husband who emerged as "the boss." With his death, she confesses, she was scared out of her mind. "It wasn't easy facing the employees [mostly men], feeling that they didn't think I was up to the job," she says.

But Shlepper's meant a lot to her, and with the support of these very employees, she's created changes, taking the business to new heights. She leads forty-five employees in three offices in the Bronx, Queens, and Manhattan. "Leadership for me didn't come from a place of comfort," she says. "It was hard work and hard-won."

Lois delivered to her team what all good leaders do: commitment. Her once skeptical employees jumped on board because they shared her passion to keep the business alive. Once her employees unified behind her, she was able to bring in new ideas.

Defining the Means for the Job

Once a leader has determined what it is that needs to happen, the second round of decisions is related to how to make it happen. To make these decisions a leader gathers information, reads the signals, and looks for patterns—it's that intuition thing! After all, to predict a certain outcome, you not only have to look at the big picture but you've got to see how the pieces fit together.

Even the best forecaster can never have complete knowledge of the future. I personally don't think business—or life for that matter—would hold any excitement with complete predictability. Sure, it's true that if we never had any doubts, we'd never be faced with having to make tough decisions. But we'd never have any choices either. And though making decisions always entails saying good-bye to at least one choice, that's where our control over our lives begins. It's the uncertainty about the future that keeps us awake in the present.

This is not to say that being aware of what's happened in the past isn't an important component of good decision-making. And an active intuition supplies the muscle for this part. But it is self-knowledge that gives us the emotional free-dom to tailor-make the best fitting decisions. This is where our passion unlocks hidden compartments of our minds. Good leaders look honestly at themselves with the courage to see their weaknesses. They know themselves well—inside and out. This is important because to get any job off to a good start, a leader's first task is to set out to complement her strengths and compensate for her shortcomings.

I'm my own best example. I know that I'd rather deal with a mile-long line of irate customers than have to prepare a financial statement or franchise tax report (though I can read them upside down and backward). So, it's no coincidence that the first employee I set out to hire was (is) an accounting guru.

There's no way that Gracie Perez could have known how eager I was to pass the baton of counting the money on to someone else when she applied for the position.

Even before we got into the nitty-gritty of her experience during her interview, she told me that she was four months pregnant. The only reason she was in the job market was that her employer had suddenly decided to close shop and she had been the last employee to be laid off.

I was impressed with how forthcoming she was about her situation. Never mind that she would barely be getting her feet wet when she'd be taking maternity leave. And forget about the possibility that she might make her leave of absence more permanent. Her integrity, her dedication to her previous employer, and her résumé gave me all the reasons I needed to hire her on the spot.

Immediately, we were like strings of a violin vibrating in unison. While in the hospital between labor pains, she called to—get this—help me prepare a financial statement. Gracie's little girl, Amanda, and my business were born the same year. It makes for a wonderful annual celebration.

It was my self-knowledge that created the opportunity for me to make my first hiring decision a good one. Not only did I know that an accountant should be the first person brought on board, but I had a good sense of what trait I considered most valuable for the position—trustworthiness. Realizing that there is no such thing as a perfect solution, I accepted some risk with my decision. I took what I knew about myself and made the decision that best fit me in my new role as a leader.

I have learned not to be afraid or embarrassed to admit what I don't know and yield to people who know better. I believe that because women generally have more of a willingness to express their vulnerabilities, we're naturals at finding ways to close the gap between what needs to be done and what we either can't do or would rather not do.

In the case of Lurita Doan, founder and president of New Technology Management, Inc., in Virginia, it was a matter of playing to a strength she knew she had. Starting her business on Halloween, because "it was a scary thing to do," as she says, she set forth in her business plan *not* to have all the answers. She knew that she was good at cleanup; therefore, she consciously implemented plans she knew were less than perfect, which played to her strengths.

With her company now delivering on contracts valued at more than $25 million and enjoying a growth rate of 4,000 percent, it's obvious Lurita has applied her self-knowledge very well.

But as strong as women seem to be at applying self-knowledge about their shortcomings and strengths to business start-ups, I often see women having a problem with delegating. Too often, women in a position of authority are either reluctant or unwilling to let others do the work for which they are being paid. I believe this kind of hold-my-cards-close-to-my-chest response stems from a low self-esteem. A fear of not being needed is at the heart of this kind of behavior, which causes a woman not to want to share responsibilities.

We've all heard it said, "If you want the job done right, you have to do it yourself." That is probably one of the most paralyzing clichés of all times. The fear that someone might think less of us if we do less is linked to our relationship-based self-identification.

And yes, it takes one to know one. One of the hardest things I've ever done in business is to hand a job over to someone else. From opening mail to greeting every customer personally, I felt that if I let go of any of it, I would look bad in someone's eyes. My fear of disapproval—from anyone on the planet—eliminated the word "delegate" from my vocabulary for longer than I care to admit.

Then the day came when I woke up and didn't *want* to go to work. I was resentful of the many people that needed me. Yet I had created the monster. "Can't they do *anything* without me?" I'd ask myself. Well, of course they couldn't. That's the system I had created. And it stifled their growth and by extension impaired the health of my companies. Not to mention that there was no time for my personal and professional development. I was too busy doing the same things over and over.

Jessica, another woman who learned the importance of delegating, works at a high-level position in an insurance company. Frustration led her to enroll in a management class in order to sharpen her leadership skills and take her career to the next level. It was there that she learned that she had been stifled by wanting to be popular with everyone—her review committee, her peers, and her employees. She learned that this desire was causing her to shoulder more responsibility than she actually should. She felt like she had to play mom to everyone. This I'm-the-only-one-for-the-job style had even gained her recognition in the past. It's no wonder she kept using it.

When the management class ended and she returned to work armed with new realizations and tools, her first decision was to create change, naming people to new positions and creating stronger support systems. No longer was everyone dependent on her for the support they needed.

Knowing that people are typically resistant to change, the next thing she did was meet with her new captains. She shot "straight between the eyes," as she tells it, and told them that their positions were created to help them all grow and perform without her. Before taking the course, she says she never would have told them that for fear of causing them to feel abandoned. And of course, then they might be mad at her.

Upon full implementation of the new human resources structure, her career soared and so did the bottom line of the business. She had become more valuable to the insurance company but also—because she was able to personally explore the land of the unfamiliar—she experienced an enhanced self-worth.

I always try to remind myself that self-development is the one thing I can't delegate. That helps me to let go of other things. Time and again I've seen evidence that to delegate appropriately is the best means of getting the job done.

Motivating the Players

You're only as good as the people you hire.

—RAY KROC, FOUNDER,

McDONALD'S CORPORATION

Hiring the right people is a critical responsibility with which leaders are charged. Yet, too often it's a responsibility that isn't given its due respect.

Some say that Ray Kroc set the standard for modern business leadership. He had a concept for the restaurant business that was and is employee-intensive. After opening his first hamburger joint in 1955, he continued to expand by introducing his franchise system. He accomplished quite a feat, not just by creating a recipe for fabulous French fries (my weakness), but also by creating opportunities for other people. Creating a work environment where allegiance works two ways, where a vision is shared, and where people are allowed to realize their full potential is challenging but rewarding.

It all starts in the hiring. And be aware: Your employees are watching your hiring practices. If you typically hire anyone who can walk, talk, and chew gum at the same time, you're in effect telling your people that they're not worth much to you. That works the other way around too.

The goal achieved by making all of the right hiring decisions is to walk in every morning and see progress, to smile at your employees and have them smile back at you—both of you enthusiastic and sharing the same dream. Let's at least accept this scenario as the desired ideal. After all, we all have a little Pollyanna in us.

In order for this dream scene to ever come close to reality, you'll have to place a great deal of importance on keeping employees. Because women are relationship-oriented (even in the eyes of all the male experts), this aspect of leadership is one that looms large in a lady boss's playbook.

Retaining the people that you've hired can be compared to a marriage. It takes work. It takes nurturing. I'm reminded of the old couple who had been married forty years who went to see a marriage counselor. "What brings you two here?" the counselor asked.

"He never tells me that he loves me," the wife responded.

"I told you the day I married you. If that had changed, I would have let you know," the husband shot back.

In the end, this couple was able to save their marriage because they opened up a new artery of communication. To motivate my employees to aim at the same target, I involve them in telling me what they want and need. After all, it's a communication challenge to be able to get people to embrace change. Selling your decisions to others—decisions that may generate controversy and discomfort—demands every one of your strengths. I've learned from my own employees that there are five basic tenets that people consider essential to their positive work experience: development of talents and abilities, appreciation, rules applied consistently, a sense of belonging, and fair compensation. According to my own exit interviews, the number one reason that employees cross the street is lack of interesting work. Employees want and need challenges. The ability to develop others is a prime leadership responsibility.

As one executive woman told me, "Every time I've ever received a promotion, I was told that it was because I knew how to maximize people's strengths." She tells how important it is to create stretch opportunities for people. "Appropriate stress is more important than appropriate dress," she says. "Everyone likes to get butterflies in their stomach now and then." Watch employees' eyes light up when you tell them that you need and will provide the means for them to learn a new skill. People want to learn. They want to be more valuable to the team.

While they're learning, be sure to give them permission to fail. I try to remind myself that failures are fertilizers for accomplishments. Entrepreneur Terri Bowersock tells how she placed an executive in the field to negotiate a lease. He pushed the negotiation too far and lost the deal. She asked him if he had learned from his mistake. When he told her that indeed he had, she said, "Good, you're now ready for this tough one." She tells her story with a happy ending. "He became a great negotiator. He failed fast."

The old adage "If you don't take care of them, someone else will" was probably coined with customers in mind, but who ever heard of miserable employees making for happy customers?

Showing appreciation takes a conscious effort. I've learned how important it can be to write a simple note of thanks for some good deed. A couple of movie tickets as a gesture of work well done or a good old-fashioned pat on the back have worked wonders. Underled or misled businesses almost always have a crew of unappreciated employees.

Along with opportunities for personal development and a clear sense of being appreciated, employees want rules. Even as a parent I lean toward leniency, so this tenet was a tough one for me to grasp. With my sensitivity in overdrive, I had a desire to be thought of as a "cool boss," just like I wanted to be a "cool mom." But when it finally registered on me that good morale and discipline go hand in hand, I was able to crown more achievements—theirs and mine.

Kathy Sanchez of Albuquerque said that in her computer firm of eighteen employees, she was reluctant to discipline her employees for fear of coming off as being "too masculine." The more I asked the big discipline question of female executives, the more I recognized a common thread running through the female style: Disciplining employees is not a favorite of female bosses.

Deborah Naybor, a surveying company entrepreneur, says that because female entrepreneurs are somewhat maverick themselves, rule making is often the last thing they want to spend time doing. Everyone I talked to agreed though: Rules make people feel safe and secure. Rules and discipline give people a sense of common purpose. The trick is to enforce them fairly and with consistency. A woman who acquiesces to everyone else's opinions and yields to their every wish is accepting temporary relief and ignoring potential catastrophe.

Naybor also added that she's learned how important it is to have some flexible guidelines in place to which employees can refer to when no detailed instructions exist. In the military, they're sometimes referred to as standing orders. Whenever I'm considering making an exception, I often refer to the spirit of the company rules in my meetings. But I'm always conscious of consistency. If the exceptions are allowed to become the rules, your ability to lead is sure to erode.

A sense of belonging also rated in the top five most important concerns according to my company's annual employee survey. This is where feedback is so important. Everyone wants to know, "How am I doing?" Scheduled job evaluations are important but don't let them be in lieu of walking/talking spontaneous feedback and direction. Too many leaders lead by remote control. Even in politics, leaders know the value of "pressing the flesh." A business, or any kind of relationship for that matter, is like a living organism in need of nurturing and encouragement.

Create a workplace where your people—whether one or one thousand—are made to feel appreciated. Help them to be the best that they can be. Create and enforce commonsense rules and guidelines and give them a sense of belonging and you've got the top four of the five most important issues to employees covered. Number five? Pay them honestly and competitively and you're on you way to having one big happy family.

Am I a leader? Yes. But, I wasn't born one. Are you a leader? Contrary to all this psychological testing that we read about today, there's no absolute way to find out until you try it. But you can begin by asking yourself: Do I have a reason or a purpose for doing something? Do I possess the means to get it done? Am I capable of motivating a team? The answers don't have to be one hundred percent unqualified yes, but if you can see the vision, evenly faintly, then I would say, yes, you are a "natural born" leader.

Through my own experiences and those of the women who have shared their stories with me, I've observed that most of us do not separate our professional and personal selves as clearly and cleanly as men tend to. It goes back to the earlier discussion about how men and women define themselves. And when it comes to leadership roles, the real challenge for most women is how they can achieve success in business without losing the rest of what they consider to be important.

eleven

Balance

Having "more leisure time" is the number-one way to improve our lives in this new millennium. That's according to North American women included in the 2000 Global Women's Survey, which polled 30,000 women in thirty-three countries around the world on issues ranging from women in business and life challenges to beauty, health, and fitness. A very close second, according to the survey, is the "ability to be financially independent."

Exploring the issue of financial independence further, the survey also asked, "What three factors would make it easier for a woman to start her own business?" According to the survey, the support of a spouse/domestic partner is the leading factor that would facilitate becoming an entrepreneur. (Curiously, the second enabling factor globally is more self-confidence. The third factor is having a large network of personal contacts.)

What is extremely compelling about the results of this survey, but perhaps not surprising, is how the personal and professional lives of women are invariably linked," said Susan Kropf, chief operating officer, Avon North America and Global Business Operations.

I've walked the tightrope of trying to balance a career and family in my own life. There were times I questioned my own identity. Sometimes, in the quiet hours of a sleepless night I would feel so isolated, complaining to my pillow that there couldn't be another woman so put upon as I was feeling. Just learning that tens of thousands of other women shared this plight helped me to find the courage to keep going. Many of their inspiring stories have animated this book.

Paying the Price

Times have changed. Paths have been cleared. Opportunities are greater. But, so is the confusion.

Young women today have so many more choices in work and life, yet they are suffering more than ever from anxiety-related disorders. Drawing a new road map and creating a meaningful life seems to be much more difficult for young women now. They may be talking "choice" but they're thinking "dilemma." They know that the choices they make today may come with a high price tomorrow.

A twenty-seven-year-old stockbroker I talked to confessed one of her deepest fears: "I'm so focused on my career. I worry that all the good guys will be taken by the time I decide I'm ready for one." (I'll bet that no man ever asked the question: "Will all the good women be gone when I'm ready to settle down?")

I've received a lot of credit during my career for being a good role model, but honestly, when I started out, the idea of being a role model for anyone was the furthest thing from my mind. I've broken down some barriers and I've enjoyed many firsts. But when I examine why I did it, I can't claim that I set out to make the corporate world more female-friendly for the next generation.

Nor was I simply trying to fulfill my potential. I was trying to survive. I wasn't seeking financial or any other kind of independence. There was nothing independent about my life. That would have been a luxury. I had two small mouths to feed. My sons needed me. I had to make money. But unlike most men, I didn't have a wife to provide me with a comfortable home life. (The Avon Survey called it "support of a spouse or domestic partner.")

I believe that there are two significant advantages that

have enabled men to hang on to their preeminent place in business. Number one: Although the studies and numbers vary, it's a safe assumption that the vast majority of men in high-ranking business positions have a source of domestic support. Conversely, the majority of women who hold these same positions, like myself, do not. Number two: Men set out to make money from the get go. Sons are admonished to pursue whatever makes them money—and whatever allows them to fulfill the traditional role of breadwinner. Daughters are encouraged to pursue whatever makes them happy and, more often than not, that means creating satisfying relationships. In truth money and happiness need not be exclusive of one another.

Early in life, boys are taught to think in terms of financial success. Girls think in terms of fulfillment. Heaven forbid that a girl should invest time and money in education and work experience, preparing her to be a high-powered executive, and then "waste" it by coming off her career path to have children. Young men are not merely encouraged, they are driven to have clear visions about their careers. Young women are told they can be anything they want to be—as long as they promise to take care of others along the way. It's a tough gig.

Young women today have got to be told the truth. There are prices to be paid for professional success. *All* women in business careers have made sacrifices.

Whatever destinations you choose to plot on your map, know that no woman can survive if she is all over the map.

But the surest way to go nowhere is to allow yourself to be paralyzed by indecisiveness. Choices have a way of morphing into confusion. Don't let them. Consider that entrepreneurship, while not a perfect solution, can bring about financial empowerment. And more important, it can eventually give you the flexibility that will let you find the fulfillment through family, friends, and other interests that you deserve.

Balancing Our Inner Selves

Whenever we talk about balance in our lives, women generally focus on the need for more time to fulfill our many roles. Too often both women and men are distracted by focusing on the traditional gender roles from achieving true balance in their lives. The real challenge is to balance the masculine and feminine sides of our natures rather than trying to juggle the demands put upon us by society and history.

When we're able to embrace all of our qualities, then we are able to stitch together a whole life. This lack of wholeness, or a lack of appreciation for all aspects of our true selves, is the worst adversary of healthy self-esteem and by extension inner balance.

When I joined the ranks of the male-dominated automotive industry, I learned quickly which human qualities were most valued—and they were traditionally masculine. In the beginning, I imitated many of these qualities by creating a carefully constructed facade. I took great pride in being referred to as "one of the guys." I learned to talk like them, pitch a sale like them, and compete—not only with them but also like them. In short, I distanced myself from my feminine side. I even communed with the guys in such a way that I joined their disapproval of "weak" people—particularly women. It's no wonder that their approval followed. After all, imitation is the sincerest form of flattery.

I suppose in my extraordinary situation, having just lost a breast and my ability to have children, as well as seeing my marriage fall apart, I was struggling to keep control. My lack of self-love took me way off balance. My "femininity" was being sacrificed for the esteemed masculine virtues I borrowed from the men with whom I worked. It was almost as though I needed to compensate for the losses, the pain of rejection, and a sense of failure. I was becoming the man I wanted to have love me. In the end, my new family of friends unknowingly guided me to an important self-discovery: Most of the pressure I was feeling was self-induced.

Women in their search for a magic rescue—in a fervent search for true inner balance—look in many places for their completion. For me, it was a distorted gender mask. For some, it's romantic relationships. For some, it's addictions. For many, it's sacrificing our own needs to the needs of others. We become compulsive helpers.

In truth, no one or nothing can give to you the rest of your self.

It was only when I realized that I possessed unique versions of many "masculine qualities," that I discovered an inner self where my femininity could come alive. A whole woman—or a whole man for that matter—is one who has her masculine and feminine side perfectly blended. When the vigor of our strengths meets the vulnerability of our weaknesses, we're able to enjoy inner balance.

Setting Priorities—One Day at a Time

For the most part, women have come to learn that balance doesn't mean that everything and everyone get equal time and equal consideration everyday. Picture a teeter-totter. The object of this playground game is to prevent either end from completely touching the ground. It's okay that one end may be higher than the other. The dynamic interplay of forces and energy doesn't allow both seats to be suspended in the air at equal distances from the ground all the time. Such is balance between career and family.

While I'm not going to judge whether family or career is more important for any individual, it's hard to imagine that any woman—or man for that matter—ever wished on her deathbed for "just one more business deal." In fact, if you heed all of the principled career advice out there—if you operate your business with all of the vision, passion, and focus you can muster—there will be many days when your business will eat up the better part of your time, attention, and energy.

Setting priorities isn't always as easy as deciding whether to go home and bake cupcakes for little Timmy's school bake sale or to stay at work and clean up your Rolodex. Our own hunger for a better life means we sometimes go hungry for the basics in life. We leverage our*selves* for the sake of getting ahead.

I recall when I first moved to Corpus Christi, Texas, to start my own business. Equipped with a four-and-a-half-year résumé, a few business accolades, a start-up loan from a risk-taking investor, and a blessed naiveté, I was now a CEO. I was undaunted by the fact that I had no product to sell, no building, no furnishings, and no equipment. My intuition told me what I needed most was new friends. I had to create a support group. And so I joined. I joined every club, association, committee, and task force that would have me.

No stranger to being the new girl on the block (I attended ten different schools in three states in twelve years), I knew it was going to take a lot of giving to gain acceptance. Within two years, I was serving—not just sitting on—eleven boards and attending fifteen to twenty community service functions per week! (One day I walked in to pay a goodwill visit to the local women's shelter and walked out as the chairman of the new building campaign.) Like so many communities, South Texas is one that embraces its do-gooders. I basked in it.

Acquaintances? Connections? My Rolodex was so full

that it was begging for mercy. Close friends? Too few. My own mother had to call my office to arrange an appointment just to speak to me. Imagine what it took for her to have lunch with me. I had been sharing, serving, volunteering, and giving. The word "No" was not part of my vocabulary.

It took seven years before it hit me. I had let the work side of my teeter-totter get way too heavy—even though the journey downward was exhilarating and professionally satisfying. It was time to push off again to bring my family and myself back into play.

I had been thrust into the workforce by circumstances beyond my control before I had been able to finish drawing my own life map. As a result, I had to navigate some rocky terrain unguided—and did so at a pretty breakneck pace. My sons, by extension, made sacrifices too. We're still sorting through some of the damage. But love has been and still is our compass.

I'd venture to say that kids today are even empathizing with their parents. Elizabeth Hunter, an active seventeen-year-old in Decorah, Iowa, says that she feels for her mom trying to do it all. "It's like if she doesn't come to my soccer match, she thinks she's a bad mom," she says.

Many of the decisions we have to make will call for quick judgments. Many times your choices will have negative consequences. We hear a lot about competing priorities but what about competing crises?

For Natalie, a divorcée in her late thirties with a troubled teenager and a troubled printing business, the clash between the two aspects of her life came to a head with a call from the local police department one night while she was working late in her small printing company. The arresting officer told her that her teenage son had been "busted" at a football game for possession of alcohol. Her first instinct was to leave her son in police custody until she could get past her immediate work crisis, but her choice wasn't that simple. The officer told her that if she came to get him now, he'd forgo the arrest proceedings. But she knew that if she shut down her presses, she'd surely miss her deadline. Knowing that she had no one to turn to at work, she asked the officer if he could just "hold" her son a couple of hours. His reply felt like a knife stabbing right into her heart. "No wonder this kid's got problems. You don't care."

In the end, she had mercy on her son, yet she was unable to bail herself out of her business jam. Her son had violated the law and, in missing her deadline, she had violated the terms of a contract.

Take Time for Yourself

Cathy is her family's sole breadwinner and the primary caregiver of her twelve-year-old invalid son, Terry. Everyday for many months she had been chauffeuring her son to a nearby clinic for a new therapy. On top of her regular job, she had been taking on secretarial work at home to pay the extra medical costs not covered by insurance. When her daughter, who had been away at college, came home for the holidays, she was appalled by her mother's appearance. Cathy's sallow complexion and the dark circles under her eyes spoke volumes. Working full time, doing extra work at night, eating poorly, getting no exercise, and functioning on four to five hours sleep a night, Cathy had lost all sense of personal fulfillment as she tended to her son's needs and those of her employer and clients.

The first warning that she was running on empty came when she lost a client due to too many errors in her work. Then she sprained her ankle doing regular housework. Now her daughter was telling her flat out, "Mom, you've got to change something here. Terry's condition has not improved and you're a mess. Please Mom, you've got to start taking care of you! You're killing yourself and we need you to be around for a while." From her daughter's plea, Cathy learned a vital lesson. Our own well-being is as important to those we love as what we do for them.

In our efforts to be superwomen, we tend to fill every minute of every day with some kind of something. When we turn the page of a calendar, it looks like a Jackson Pollock painting. It's no wonder we suffer from battle fatigue.

By nature, women possess incredible stamina, fueled by passion and resilience. I believe that we can pretty much do it all—for a while. But then exhaustion sets in that can result in incompetence and even illness. Our bodies and our minds will force us to surrender to tiredness if we don't do it on our own.

If you're someone who pays attention to the signals your mind and body give you—a headache, a backache, slight confusion, eye fatigue, or forgetfulness—I applaud you. If you're more likely to ignore those signals and keep on going, you'll want to take heed of Cathy's story and figure out a way to stay in the race without losing your soul.

Self-Reliance

With all due respect to those who believe that having the support of their partner and family is their key to achieving balance, I submit that women have to look to themselves *first*. We sacrifice personal time, personal development, and even sleep all in the name of taking care of others. Putting the same time and effort into taking care of ourselves, won't unbalance our partnerships or our lives—it does just the opposite.

Each one of us has a huge stake in the design of our own lives. If we do not create ways to replenish depleted energy, we're sure to risk burnout. I think of it as a crime of passion because burnout often leads to depression, and passion and depression are not compatible partners. When we sacrifice who we are—and the potential for what we can become—all in the name of nurturing others, a sense of imbalance is the result. I've learned that I deserve more than just the scraps that are leftover after I give all of the other pieces of myself away.

Reconciling the many parts of our lives begins with an appreciation of the true meaning of balance. What I have gleaned from my work inside a predominately male industry is that a human quality is a human quality. Achieving internal wholeness—one that allows us to love ourselves as we love others—will serve a larger purpose. In the grand scheme of things, change inside the business world and in society at large is possible, and rich in potential for both sexes. When men and women accept and share each other's strengths, they will create a support system to make a well-balanced life a possibility for everyone.